Unforgettable
UTAH

Historic Moments, Milestones & Marvels

LYNN ARAVE

THE
History
PRESS

Published by The History Press
Charleston, SC
www.historypress.com

Copyright © 2024 by Lynn Arave
All rights reserved

Cover images: courtesy of Utah State Historical Society.

First published 2024

Manufactured in the United States

ISBN 9781467155489

Library of Congress Control Number: 2023947111

Notice: The information in this book is true and complete to the best of our knowledge. It is offered without guarantee on the part of the author or The History Press. The author and The History Press disclaim all liability in connection with the use of this book.

To Newspapers.com, where "time travel" is possible, and so is this new book, thanks primarily to their sources.

CONTENTS

CONTENTS

ACKNOWLEDGEMENTS

Many thanks to Newspapers.com and Utah Digital Newspapers for their extensive and easy-to-search archives.

Special credit to all the sources that allowed use of their historical images for this book. These include the following: the Utah State Historical Society, the J. Willard Marriott Digital Library at the University of Utah, the Library of Congress, Brigham Young University Lee Library, Wikipedia Commons, the Church of Jesus Christ of Latter-day Saints, *Deseret News* archives, *Salt Lake Tribune* archives, Ruby's Inn, Ogden City, D. Boyd Crawford Photo Collection, Heritage Museum of Layton and Harold Flygare Family Photo Collection.

Friends and family who supplied pictures for this book are Ravell Call, Roger Arave, Steven Arave, LeAnn Arave and Liz Arave Hafen.

INTRODUCTION

This book is a sequel of sorts to my 2022 book, *Legends, Lore and True Tales of Utah*. It includes new material, though.

Information in this book primarily comes from old newspaper research by me. Thousands of hours were spent scouring old Utah newspapers by keywords to find some of the aspects of the state's history that are not found in standard history books. Some unexpected gems were also found accidentally during those long searches.

Many "what-ifs?" were found. These were things that could have made Utah's history slightly different or that could have substantially changed it forever.

A number of the chapters herein are also the product of exhaustive research conducted while I was employed as a full-time reporter/editor with the *Deseret News*.

Most of the information stems from my vast curiosity: who, what, when, where, why and how?

Much of the material on national park accidents comes from incident reports provided by the National Park Service.

Some of the chapters were previously published in the *Deseret News* and the *Ogden Standard-Examiner*.

Other content corresponds to my Google blog, *Mystery of Utah History* (where history buffs can read even more obscure Utah history).

I

Fabled Places

1

KANARRAVILLE FALLS

Local Secret for Decades

The Kanarraville Falls, a five-mile roundtrip hike, is the hottest scenic rage in Southwest Utah these days. Indeed, in 2023, the hike sold out for most of the summer in early May.

Fueled by Kanarra Creek, this small slot canyon, named Kanarraville Canyon, was a secret known only to locals for many decades. (Kanarraville is a small town about thirteen miles southwest of Cedar City, along I-15.)

An exhaustive newspaper search of these waterfalls reveals nothing until the twenty-first century. Indeed, "Best-Kept Secret Becomes Nightmare" was the title of a June 25, 2017 Associated Press story in the *Daily Sentinel* of Grand Junction, Colorado, and in many other western newspapers that summer.

The *Sentinel* story stated that the first time town members noticed that their little slot canyon was no longer a secret was on July Fourth weekend of 2004, when seventy-five cars were crowded into the trailhead's parking lot.

How did the community keep it secret for so long? "Very carefully," responded the ticket taker / security guard at the gate to the trailhead.

A hiker from Ohio said he was told that when the Zion Narrows were closed due to high water in 2004, the National Park Service, which knew about the smaller canyon, referred hikers to Kanarraville instead. And things took off from there. The secret was out, and social media expanded the canyon's popularity.

By the end of the 2015 hiking season, more than forty thousand people had been counted as visiting the falls. Then, Kanarraville City decided to pay for an actual parking lot at the trailhead. Eventually, it charged ten

Left: This simple metal ladder used to allow access to the upper portion of the Kanarraville trail. A new, sturdier ladder has since been installed. *Author photo*.

Opposite: The Kanarraville Falls hike boasts some narrow slot areas that rival the Virgin River Narrows in Zion National Park for beauty. *Author photo*.

dollars a person to hike the trail in order to fund various trailhead and trail improvements.

When the coronavirus struck in 2020 and Zion National Park was overloaded, adventure lovers began to look for suitable options nearby.

Kanarraville Falls is indeed a mini Zion Narrows experience.

Kanarra Creek is the town's main source of drinking water (along with a spring near the creek), and therein lies a big concern regarding pollution. Gates were placed along a road leading to the mouth of the canyon to prevent parties from being held there. In the past, some people had hauled couches and other amenities up the mountain.

In 2016, the parking lot grossed $95,500 in fees. As of 2023, the entry fee is $12 a person, and there is a limit of 150 hikers per day. Finding the trailhead is easy, as the city has road signs posted in town.

A considerable amount of scrambling is required along the upper portions of the trail. In fact, though much shorter than the Zion Narrows, the seven-

hundred-foot elevation change and the scrambling make Kanarraville a harder hike than the Narrows.

The first eight-tenths of a mile along the Kanarraville trail follows an old canyon access road and crosses the stream twice. With its ups and downs, this is a very difficult portion of the trail, in terms of endurance. The first

The second waterfall along the Kanarraville Falls Trail is about two and a half miles out. This canyon was a local secret until the twenty-first century. *Author photo*.

waterfall is one and six-tenths miles up the trail. A fifteen-foot ladder with metal rungs, but no handrails, must be scaled to continue from this point. Although it may appear challenging, the ladder is firmly secured, though nearby rushing water splashes over the ladder

At one and seven-tenths miles out is a spot with several logs and a tall boulder that must be climbed. This is where many injuries from falls have occurred on the trail. There is a rope attached to the lower portion of this spot but not to the upper part.

The second waterfall is one and nine-tenths miles up the trail. It is preceded by the narrowest section of the canyon, which also has the deepest water.

Prior to the public discovery of Kanarraville Falls, the town of Kanarraville's claim to fame was that in the early 1960s, some California residents camped near the mouth of Spring Creek, one canyon south of the Falls Canyon. The group of some twenty-six residents spent more than six years there, pioneering and living off the land.

Small gold deposits were also found in the mountains east of Kanarraville in 1939, according to the *Salt Lake Tribune* of February 3 that year. Kanarra Creek caused some flooding in town in the spring of 1912, according to the *Iron County Record* of May 17, 1912.

Kanarraville is named for a local Paiute Indian leader from the nineteenth century. This band of Native Americans frequently camped near where the town is today. Kanarraville Falls is on Bureau of Land Management terrain, though the city administers it because of watershed concerns.

No dogs are allowed on the trail. Kanarraville residents also have no priority access to the trail. They must, like everyone else, secure a reservation and pay the fee.

Even with only 150 hikers a day allowed on the trail, it can be crowded at times. And yes, accidents have happened to hikers on the Kanarraville Falls trail. "Teen Falls 60 Feet at Kanarraville Falls" was a May 16, 2013 headline in the *Daily Spectrum* newspaper of St. George. The sixteen-year-old Las Vegas boy had to be rescued out of the canyon and suffered several broken bones. The boy was attempting to hike up a slippery slope to see where the water originated above a rock.

"Injured Hiker Expressed Gratitude for Search and Rescue's Response" was an August 3, 2004 headline in the *Spectrum*. A young woman from Arizona broke her leg after falling near one of the canyon's two waterfalls.

2

BOX CANYON

Geological Delight

S anpete County in Utah boasts a magnificent slot canyon that is still relatively unknown.

Box Canyon, an offshoot of Maple Canyon, southwest of Fountain Green and northwest of Manti, is a geographical delight and has been since it was first characterized as such in the 1930s. Indeed, an October 2, 1936 report in the *Ephraim Enterprise* stated that Snow College students annually visited Maple Canyon and especially studied the geology of Box Canyon.

Snow College professor H.R. Christensen gave students a geology lecture in Box Canyon, as its narrow width and two-hundred-foot-high canyon walls were an oddity for the area. The students also explored upper Maple Canyon, which contains an arch. Their visit was concluded with a bonfire program and a cookout.

Finding Box Canyon can be tricky. To best locate it, drive eight-tenths of a mile up Maple Canyon after the pavement ends and then park on either side of the "washboard" road. Walk less than one hundred yards up the dirt road and look north for the almost hidden entrance to Box Canyon. After you cross a small stream, you enter the slot canyon.

Box Canyon contains conglomerate rock and features a lot of scrambling opportunities over giant boulders. The canyon walls also contain some pitons, evidence that advanced rock climbers have scaled the walls there.

The canyon is rocky and usually dry. It ends about six hundred yards up, where in early spring or during wet spells a sparse waterfall might be flowing

Box Canyon, as seen in this 1926 picture, is an offshoot of Maple Canyon, southwest of Fountain Green and northwest of Manti. *Courtesy of Utah State Historical Society.*

down from above. Otherwise, a few wet areas in the upper canyon are all the moisture that is visible, as most of the water runs underground.

Hikers have to decide if they want to scramble up a large boulder in the upper canyon in order to continue until its end. Kids age eight and up will love all the rocks here. Younger children may need assistance over the rugged terrain.

This is the end of Box Canyon. It features two-hundred-foot-high canyon walls, narrow slots and conglomerate rock. *Author photo.*

To reach Box Canyon, go to Fountain Green, Utah. This small town is east of Nephi's middle I-15 exit. In Fountain Green, turn right on 400 South (west) and then head south down West Side Drive. You will pass through the extremely small towns of Freedom and Jerusalem. After about six miles, there is a prominent sign for a turnoff to Maple Canyon. The road then curves by several turkey farms before entering Maple Canyon.

3

SALT LAKE TEMPLE

Extreme Symbolism

The forty years of labor it took to construct the Salt Lake Temple—much of it without the help of machines—have come to symbolize the extreme dedication, sacrifice, self-reliance and faith possessed by early members of the Church of Jesus Christ of Latter-day Saints in Utah. The exterior, like the interior, of the iconic structure contains a wealth of symbols and representations.

"Notable among all LDS temples, the Salt Lake Temple includes significant symbolism in its architecture," the Encyclopedia of Mormonism states. The temple "stands as an isolated mass of the everlasting hills." Elder James E. Talmage wrote in *The House of the Lord*, "As nearly as any work of man may so do, It suggests duration."

While it would be improper to discuss the inside of the sacred temple's symbolism, the outside of the edifice has been publicly written about over the years, as anyone can view that aspect. What follows are examples of the temple's extensive exterior symbolism.

Granite. While LDS temple buildings generally represent mountains, which in ancient times were climbed for solitude and private communion with a deity, the Salt Lake Temple has more symbolism than any other. The gray granite walls symbolize the enduring and eternal nature of the ordinances performed therein and of the everlasting hills.

The granite for the temple came from the mountain walls in Little Cottonwood Canyon, southeast of Salt Lake City. Deep excavations around

An 1892 photo showing an almost completed Salt Lake Temple. The temple exterior has several inscriptions and numerous symbols. *Courtesy of the Brigham Young University Lee Library, L. Tom Perry Special Collection.*

The central towers on both the east and west sides of the Salt Lake Temple contain stones showing clasped hands. These symbolize the hand of fellowship. *Author photo.*

the Salt Lake Temple in 1963 revealed a fourteen-foot granite foundation atop a sixteen-foot sandstone subfoundation.

Towers. The six towers themselves signify the restoration of priesthood authority. (Religious spires in general are symbolic, because they prompt onlookers to gaze heavenward.) The three eastern towers on the temple are six feet higher than their western counterparts. As such, the eastern towers represent the three members of the church's First Presidency and the Melchizedek Priesthood. The western towers portray the Presiding Bishopric of the church and the Aaronic Priesthood.

Earth stones. These are found just above the basement of the temple and at the floor of each buttress. The thirty-six stones are believed to symbolize the spreading of the Gospel throughout the world, because they represent different portions of the globe. They also represent the telestial kingdom, the lowest of the three degrees of heavenly glory in LDS beliefs.

Moon stones. These are found just above the temple's promenade and represent the moon in all its different phases. Drawings by the temple's architect, Truman O. Angell, are based on all phases of the moon during 1878. That year, there were thirteen new moons, thirteen first quarters, twelve full moons and twelve last quarters. Midway along the north wall of the temple is the first quarter of the moon, based on January 1878. The moon's phases for that year continue clockwise in sequence. The moon also represents the middle degree of glory, the terrestrial kingdom in LDS scripture.

Some people also believe that the moon's phases represent man's mortal journey, from birth to death and from darkness to light.

Sun stones. Going upward on the temple are the sun stones, with fifty-two points per face, to represent the sun's rays. These stones were patterned after the Nauvoo, Illinois temple's sun stones. These stones also represent the highest degree of glory, the celestial kingdom in LDS theology.

Star stones. Just above the cornice of the temple are five-point star stones. The eastern towers have forty star stones. These number twelve on the central towers. They are also found on the majority of keystones. The central towers on both the east and west sides contain stones showing clasped hands. These symbolize the hand of fellowship and how Latter-day Saints should characterize brotherly love.

Cloud stones. There are only two cloud stones on the temple. They are located on the east center tower and represent the Gospel piercing through superstition and the error of the world.

Inscriptions. Just above the windows on the eastern center tower is the inscription "Holiness to the Lord" (Exodus 28:36). This is inscribed somewhere on all LDS temples. Near the windows of the east and west towers are keystones inscribed with "I Am Alpha and Omega" (Revelation 22:13). This phrase represents time and eternity and is a proclamation of He who is without beginning or end.

Constellations. Above the windows on the west central tower are representations of Ursa Major and the Big Dipper. Angell once wrote that Ursa Major and its pointer toward the North Star symbolize that the lost may find themselves by the priesthood.

Eye. Above the upper windows in each of the center towers is a carved emblem, the "all-seeing eye."

Turrets. On the corner tower are single spire stones representing flaming torches.

Angel Moroni statue. He represents the restoration of the Gospel in the latter days. Some old photographs show that a lamp was originally mounted on the crown atop Moroni's head. That light was eventually removed.

Missing features. Not all the symbolism originally planned for the Salt Lake Temple became a reality. For example, an early sketch of the temple by Angell found hanging today in Brigham Young's guest room at Cove Fort, Millard County, shows that two Angel Moroni statues, one each on the east and west ends, were initially envisioned. Only an eastern statue was ever used, for reasons unclear.

Some of Angell's drawings from 1854 show "Saturn stones," complete with rings, located directly above the sun stones. These were never placed on the temple walls.

For perhaps its first few decades, the Salt Lake Temple used to have statues of Joseph and Hyrum Smith, one each in niches at the top of the two eastern exterior stairways. These bronze statues were later removed

The east side of the Salt Lake Temple has an inscription panel and is topped by a golden Angel Moroni. *Author photo*.

and placed elsewhere on the temple block. The empty spaces where these two statues once stood remain and are popular photography spots for wedding parties today.

Note: The Salt Lake Temple is undergoing significant remodeling and seismic enhancements, probably into the year 2025, before completion.

4

ENSIGN PEAK

Utah's "Mount Sinai"

It's Utah's most sacred mountain, kind of the state's own version of Mount Sinai. At an elevation of 5,414 feet, this mound-shaped peak, named Ensign, is located behind the Utah State Capitol and is only about 1,100 feet above the city streets—far lower than most other Wasatch Mountain peaks. However, probably no other Utah mountain has a more significant religious history.

According to President George A. Smith, at one time a first counselor in the First Presidency, Brigham Young had a vision of Joseph Smith and Mount Ensign while in the Nauvoo Temple prior to leaving the East: "President Young had a vision of Joseph Smith, who showed him the mountain that we now call Ensign Peak, immediately north of Salt Lake City, and there was an ensign that fell upon that peak, and Joseph said, 'Build under that point where the colors fall and you will prosper and have peace.'"

President Joseph F. Smith provided a similar description thirteen years later. Brigham Young "had before seen an ensign descend and light upon the mountain peak, which is now called from that circumstance—'Ensign Peak'—which was an indication to him that this was the resting place God designed for His people."

The Mormon pioneers arrived in Utah on Saturday, July 24, 1847. They spent all of the next day, Sunday, resting and worshiping God. On July 26, one of the first tasks attempted was to climb what is now known as Ensign Peak to get a better look at the valley and probably also to see firsthand the mountain in President Young's vision.

Ensign Peak as it appeared from the southwest in the 1940s. Housing development had yet been built in the area, and it was just a grassy plain below. *Courtesy of Utah State Historical Society.*

Among the pioneers who made that first climb were Brigham Young, Heber C. Kimball, Willard Richards, Wilford Woodruff, George A. Smith, Ezra T. Benson, Albert Carrington and William Clayton. The party used horses to make the first two-thirds of the climb, then dismounted and went on foot.

Elder Woodruff was the first to reach the summit. President Young, still ill (and barely able to make it to the top with help), was likely the slowest climber. On top of the peak, President Young said, "Here is a proper place to raise an ensign to the nations." This is a reference to the Scriptures, where it mentions an "Ensign" (Isaiah 5:26 and Doctrine and Covenants 105:39). These scriptural references are likely the inspiration for the peak's name. They're also the source for the name of one of the Church's modern monthly magazines, *The Ensign*.

The men then reportedly unfurled an ensign of liberty to the world. What the word *ensign* means here is unclear. Perhaps the most common dictionary definition is a flag or banner, specifically a national flag. But most historians are quick to point out that despite recurring myths, there's no evidence that a U.S. flag was raised on Ensign Peak at the climax of that first climb. Another definition of the word is simply a badge or symbol, in accordance with a synonym of the word: insignia.

(The pioneers did raise a U.S. flag in the valley below as early as October 1847, a significant act, since Utah was technically still Mexican soil. The U.S. flag was definitely flown on Ensign Peak, complete with a twenty-one-gun salute, on July 24, 1897, from a special flagpole. This occurred about six months after Utah was admitted to the union and was done in commemoration of the fiftieth anniversary of the pioneers' arrival. A similar celebration was held on Ensign Peak fifty years later, in 1947.)

In a speech on July 26, 1919, Richard W. Young, president of Ensign Stake of the Church of Jesus Christ of Latter-day Saints, referred to the peak as a symbol of patriotism. In a July 27 *Salt Lake Tribune* article that year, Young said: "This peak has stood for years as proof of the patriotism of the people of Utah. For the last fifty years people have looked at this peak as an altar of patriotism."

Not long after the pioneers arrived in the Salt Lake Valley, Ensign Peak was also used for a brief period as an outdoor temple until the "Endowment House" was constructed.

Ensign Peak has also had its controversial moments. For example, on February 23, 1925, the Ku Klux Klan surprised Salt Lake residents by burning a red cross on the peak. The Klan also unexpectedly burned crosses on the peak and held an initiation ceremony less than two months later, in April 1925.

The peak and its monuments have been the target of periodic vandalism. There's an eighteen-foot monument on Ensign Peak, placed there on July 26, 1934, by the Salt Lake Ensign Stake Mutual Improvement Association.

Ensign Peak as seen through Eagle Gate on Salt Lake's State Street, with the Utah State Capitol to the right. *Author photo*.

Stones gathered from along the Mormon Trail are incorporated into the rock monument. Although many inscriptions on the monument are no longer visible, such lettering as "Kolob" and "Logan Temple" can still be made out.

Additionally, an August 19, 1946 story in the *Salt Lake Telegram* reported on the sad death of a Salt Lake girl who fell to her death off the steep cliffs located northwest of Ensign Peak. The report included a map identifying the rock cliffs directly west of Ensign Peak as being called "Hell's Hollow." A "Devil's Rock" was also identified as a part of Hell's Hollow. These colorful geological feature names seem to have been lost over the decades.

5

FOUR CORNERS

Unique Tourist Mecca

T oday, visiting the famed Four Corners, the only place where four
states of America intersect, is a convenient trip over paved roads
with ample signage. But as recently as 1957, such a trip was a
rugged and even hazardous adventure. "Obscure, Perilous Dirt Route
Trap for Intrepid Tourists" was a December 22, 1957 headline in the *Salt
Lake Tribune.*

While there was already a cement marker at the spot where the four states
meet, traveling there was the problem. The *Tribune* story stated that most
maps didn't even show a road there at the time. "The last eight miles is the
worst," the story reported. "They consist of a dirt-on-top-of-boulder stretch
with rugged stones as big as 10-gallon hats to punctuate the ride."

The story also stated that the road was narrow and a bumpy washboard
for vehicles. Also, the only sign along the road was eight miles away and
read, "Four Corners—Eight Miles." The *Tribune* reported that the road was
so bad that vehicles could easily get bogged down or lost. The story ended
by proclaiming that a gross lack of signage and a proper road is why most
residents of the Four Corners states have never been to the historic marker.

Less than five years later, the *Ogden Standard-Examiner* of September 17,
1962, stated that a new highway to the Four Corners was open and that a
new monument there had been dedicated. The governors of the four states
attended the dedication ceremony. Notwithstanding, the visitation problems
at the Four Corners continued.

The Four Corners marker, as seen from a balloon or airplane in the late 1940s, was little more than white paint. *Courtesy of Utah State Historical Society.*

Taylor Arave stands on top of the marker at the Four Corners Monument. His father, the author of this book, chronicles the visit. *Author photo.*

"At Four Corners. Needed: Visitor Center, Park" was the title of an editorial in the *Provo Daily Herald* on July 6, 1972. A decade later, on May 19, 1982, the *Herald* declared, "Four Corners 'Incredible Disgrace'—Lawmakers." At that time, there were no water, toilets or cleanliness at the unique geographical site.

The situation eventually improved at Four Corners. Although the site remains in a remote area, there is plenty of signage and reasonable facilities for visitors.

6

WILLARD BASIN

Rugged Mountain Oasis

illard Peak and Willard Basin comprise some of the highest and most rugged territory in Box Elder County. Willard Basin, approximately 8,600 feet in elevation and on the back side of both Willard and Ben Lomond Peaks, is a remote oasis and has been the site of some unusual events over the decades.

For example, the *Ogden Standard-Examiner* of July 22, 1948, chronicled that Willard Basin was the site of a Jim Bridger Mountain Man Festival for some years each summer. The twelve-mile road from Mantua into the basin was widened and improved before the event. "Those making the trip will be especially fortunate in that there are hundreds of acres of wild flowers in bloom at present, with hundreds of varieties to see," the *Standard* stated.

To lessen traffic problems along the mountainous road to the basin, those going up had to be there by 11:30 a.m. on festival day. The rest of the day was reserved for return traffic on the road, so narrow in places that it is a one-lane path. The festival included races, a log-sawing contest, games and talks on geology and botany.

The *Standard-Examiner* of June 24, 1956, included the legend that Bridger himself visited the basin on the way to Willard Peak to prove that the Great Salt Lake was an arm of the ocean, since it was so salty. Bridger supposedly carved his name on a tree in the basin, though no one has been able to locate it.

A group of unidentified Weber County residents on top of Ben Lomond Peak on August 26, 1937. The group also likely peered down into the adjacent Willard Basin. *Courtesy of Utah State Historical Society.*

On September 27, 1970, the paper reported that a lofty wedding was held in the basin. Rodney L. George and Connie K. Eldredge tied the knot there, with eighteen people in attendance—all overdressed for a serene mountainous setting.

According to the *Standard-Examiner* of February 2, 1941, the original road into the basin was built by the Civilian Conservation Corps (CCC) from 1936 to 1940. Fire control, maintaining livestock fences and erosion control were the main reasons for the road's construction. (Many mountain roads in the West were built by the CCC.)

In fact, an early fall snowstorm on October 18, 1938, trapped fifteen CCC workers in Willard Basin. Bulldozers had to slowly chew their way to rescue the men, the *Standard-Examiner* of that date stated.

Willard Peak, elevation 9,763 feet, is the highest point in Weber County (taller than 9,712-foot Ben Lomond Peak), as it straddles the Box Elder–Weber County line. Paragliders have from time to time descended from Willard Peak or Ben Lomond Peak during various celebrations. For example, the town of Willard's July Fourth celebration of 1975 included paragliders jumping off Willard Peak and landing in town.

There is a small lake at the south end of Willard Basin. This entire area is most often visited by ATV users, who drive the rugged fourteen-mile dirt road. *Author photo.*

On Saturday, September 29, 1923, the schools in Box Elder County sponsored a hike to Willard Peak, the *Box Elder County News* of September 25 reported.

"500 Trek to Willard Peak" was a July 18, 1939 headline in the *Standard-Examiner*. Residents from Ogden to Brigham City hiked to the top of Willard Peak that day. Government trucks provided transportation up to Willard Basin, so the hike was only several miles long.

Who was the first non–Native American to hike Ben Lomond Peak, the most distinctive peak in Weber County? It may have been mountain man Osborne Russell in 1840. The *Standard-Examiner* of February 15, 1976, reported that Russell's diary stated that he climbed a peak on the northeast shore of the Great Salt Lake. Some believe that summit was Ben Lomond. "I was upwards of 6,000 feet above the level of the lake; below me was a dark abyss silent as the night of death," Russell's journal stated. He climbed Ben Lomond in February to hunt mountain sheep and bagged three. He also camped on the mountain and had an encounter with a wolverine.

Ben Lomond Peak is often believed to resemble a smiling face during certain winter periods. The *Standard-Examiner* of May 3, 1956, also claimed that the face of the peak "grows a beard" occasionally. "The top of the peak resembles a Boy Scout's hat. Two crevasses look like eyes. Later in the spring when melting continues, the Boy Scout sprouts a beard of melting snow and ice going down the front of the mountain."

II

Milestones in Utah

7

FIRST CHRISTMAS
IN UTAH TERRITORY

W ho was the first person (or persons) to celebrate Christmas in Utah? Was it (a) Miles Goodyear, in Ogden in 1845; (b) Mormon settler James Brown and company, in Ogden in 1847; (c) John C. Frémont and/or Kit Carson in 1843; or (d) none of the above?

If you answered (d), you are correct.

Surprisingly, it was a mountain man and trapper, Osborne Russell, who celebrated the holiday on December 25 first, in Weber County in 1840. (That's almost seven years before the Mormon pioneers arrived in the valley.)

Russell (1814–1892) was most famous as a political leader who later helped form the government of the State of Oregon. He kept a detailed journal of his nine years (1834–43) in the Rocky Mountains, and his account is a fascinating read that predates John C. Frémont and Kit Carson's visit in 1843 by almost three years.

He outlines his Christmas holiday as taking place near where the "Weaver" River (Weber River) empties into the Great Salt Lake. By that description, he most likely would have been in today's Hooper (or perhaps West Haven) for the holiday season.

Russell spent the holidays in an Indian lodge in the company of a Frenchman, his Native American wife and their child. In nearby accommodations were other Indians and children. "It was agreed on by the party to prepare a Christmas dinner," Russell wrote in his journal. He noted that his understanding of the French and Indian languages was helpful, as only three others knew English, and that was a pretty sketchy proficiency.

Mountain man and trapper Osborne Russell celebrated the first Christmas holiday in the Weber County area near here on December 25, 1840. *Author photo.*

At about 1:00 p.m., the group sat down to Christmas dinner "in the lodge where I staid which was the most spacious being about 36 ft. in circumference at the base with a fire built in the center," Russell wrote.

What did they eat? "The first dish that came on was a large tin pan 18 inches in diameter rounding full of Stewed Elk meat," Russell wrote of the 1840 holiday feast.

The group had found a large number of elk out west by the lake, wintering in the thickets of wood and brush by the river. "The next dish was similar to the first heaped up with boiled Deer meat (or as the Trappers would call it Venison, a term not used in the Mountains)," Russell continued.

"The third and fourth dishes were equal in size to the first containing a boiled flour pudding prepared with dried fruit accompanied by four quarts of sauce made of the juice of sour berries and sugar. Then came the cakes followed by about six gallons of strong coffee already sweetened with tin cups and pans to drink out of large chips or pieces of Bark Supplying the places of plates," Russell wrote.

He also explained that eating did not commence until the word was given by the landlady. Then, conversation was expected of all. "The principal topic which was discussed was the political affairs of the Rocky Mountains, the state of governments among the different tribes," Russell wrote.

What about after dinner? Russell ended his holiday account by stating: "Dinner being over the tobacco pipes were filled and lighted while the… [mothers]…and children cleared away the remains of the feast to one side of the lodge where they held a Sociable tite a tite over the fragments. After the pipes were extinguished, all agreed to have a frolic shooting at a mark which occupied the remainder of the day."

He remained where he was until January 1, 1841, at which time all the streams were iced over. So he moved eastward. Russell wrote that he then followed the Weber River eastward. When it forked, it went right into Weber Canyon. "The route was very difficult and in many places difficult travelling over high points of rocks and around huge precipices on a trail just wide enough for a single horse to walk in," Russell wrote of the canyon.

He likely camped in the Peterson area, where the snow was some five inches deep. It snowed another eight inches that night. The next morning, he went north over rolling hills into Ogden's Hole (today's Ogden Valley), where the snow was fifteen inches deep. He spotted a herd of one hundred elk and shot one for food. The next day, he returned to where he had spent Christmas and remained there for the rest of January.

There is much more to Russell's early account of the Ogden area, including descriptions of Fremont and Antelope Islands in the Great Salt Lake.

8

FIRST SERMON IN UTAH TERRITORY
(NOT BY BRIGHAM YOUNG!)

What was the first sermon ever delivered in Utah territory? According to the *Salt Lake Telegram* newspaper of July 24, 1921, it was given by Apostle Orson Pratt on July 24, 1847, soon after the first group of pioneers arrived in the Salt Lake Valley. Elder Pratt based his talk on two verses from the Book of Isaiah in the Old Testament, chapter 52, verses 7–8:

> *How beautiful upon the mountains are the feet of him that bringeth good tidings, that publisheth peace; that bringeth good tidings of good, that publisheth salvation; that saith unto Zion, Thy God reigneth!*
>
> *Thy watchmen shall lift up the voice; with the voice together shall they sing: for they shall see eye to eye, when the Lord shall bring again Zion.*

Elder Orson Pratt gave the first recorded religious sermon in Utah territory on July 24, 1847. *Courtesy of the Church of Jesus Christ of Latter-day Saints.*

(LDS Church president Brigham Young was too ill that day to give a discourse and made only a few comments after Elder Pratt's sermon.)

Pratt's discourse was an inspiration to the pioneers, as they had all safely made the trek to the Salt Lake Valley. And on July 24, 1921, some Church members met in Parley's Canyon (named after Pratt's older brother, Parley) and held a campfire reunion to honor Orson Pratt and other pioneers. Many of this group were descendants of Pratt himself.

9

FIRST RECORDED EARTHQUAKE
IN UTAH

The first recorded earthquake in the Territory of Utah might have happened in the summer of 1859. According to the *Deseret News* of September 21, 1859, residents of Parowan and Virgin City felt "a slight shock of an earthquake....It caused furniture to move and dishes to rattle....To a person lying upon the ground it appeared as if a wagon was rolling rapidly nearby."

In the same account, residents of Parowan claimed they saw "a beautiful display of the aurora borealis." On a cloudless night, they saw a broad red arch rising in the north. This took place on the night of August 31 and September 1, 1859.

Another earthquake took place in the early fall of 1868 at Fort Ephraim in San Pete County. Three distinct shocks were felt by residents, as recorded in the *Deseret News* of October 21, 1868.

On December 6, 1871, Cedar City residents reported in the *Salt Lake Herald Republican* of

A *Deseret News* article from September 21, 1859, reporting on the first recorded earthquake in Utah Territory. *Deseret News Archives.*

December 7, 1871, about feeling an "ill mannered" earthquake, which opened cupboard doors and shook large buildings. But no damage was reported.

The southern half of Utah was shaken by a series of earthquakes on November 13–14, 1901. According to the *Davis County Clipper*, people were driven from their homes and took shelter on the streets, making fires to keep warm. Some buildings in Sevier County were completely ruined. The LDS Tabernacle in Richfield suffered at least $2,000 in damages. Many buildings in Monroe required $25 to $100 to repair. The epicenter of the quakes may have been in the high Tushar Mountains, east of Beaver.

10

METEOROLOGICAL FIRSTS IN UTAH

T he *Salt Lake Herald Republican* of August 22, 1873, reported that a tornado passed over the mining town of Bingham that day. Some destruction of property was reported, and the tornado was described as "terrible."

The so-called tornado produced a lot of dust. A quick cloudburst followed, and the rain washed out three miles of railroad grade.

Strong canyon winds plagued the Utah Territory numerous times since the pioneers settled there. As the May 23, 1914 *Ogden Standard-Examiner* recalled, the windy day of November 15, 1860, brought a "Big blow" out of Ogden Canyon. It was one of the worst such winds. "Every fence that faced the wind is prostrated," the account stated. "Mr. McQuarrie's fine two-story house is leveled to the ground. Mr. Bowman's dwelling house is blown down. Mr. Jost's cottage is completely destroyed. Mr. Jonathan Browning's large two-story house—with basement for mercantile purposes, as also that house of M.C. Shurtliff."

Ogden City Hall was unroofed. About one-third of the north side of the tabernacle was also unroofed. A cow belonging to Mr. Ensign was killed when a pole from a shed came loose and hit the animal in the head.

October 20–21, 1906, saw another big blow in Ogden. "Storm Did Damage to Nearly Every House. Railroad Trains and Street Cars Failed to Move for Hours—Electric Light and Telephone Lines Damaged—There Will Be No Lights in Homes of Ogden Tonight" was the October 22, 1906 headline in the *Standard*. The report stated that hurricane-force winds blew

The First National Bank building in Layton was heavily damaged by strong canyon winds in the spring of 1905. *Courtesy of Heritage Museum of Layton.*

for thirty-six hours. Many windows were broken, and at least two hundred telephone poles were knocked down, along with many chimneys.

October 30–31, 1920, saw still another high-wind event. The November 1 *Standard* stated that trees, telephone poles and barns were damaged. A rusting city water main on Twenty-Third Street between Adams and Jefferson Avenues also broke during the storm "and caused a flood to sweep down the hill."

The pioneers soon noticed that a "cap cloud," a low-hanging cloud along the crest of Wasatch Mountains, often meant that canyon winds would follow twenty-four and seventy-two hours later.

Davis County also has a lengthy history of canyon wind events. During a visit by Brigham Young to Farmington on November 9, 1864, the canyon winds were blowing, and President Young rebuked the winds. Until 1896, the canyon winds didn't return.

But earlier, in February 1864, canyon winds struck Farmington hard during a winter cold spell. Elizabeth Rigby and her son John froze to death in that storm after being pinned against a fence by hurricane-force winds. Elizabeth's husband, John Rigby, was in Salt Lake on business at the time. Besides the two fatalities, the Rigby home's roof was blown off and some two hundred sheep, six horses and ten cows perished because of downed buildings and frigid winds.

This is canyon wind damage at a Centerville home. The winds blew hardest here on March 28, 1963, toppling part of the house. *Courtesy of Utah State Historical Society.*

The first canyon winds recorded by pioneers in Davis County happened in the fall of 1848, within the first few days of the arrival of some settlers, like Daniel A. Miller of Farmington.

Utah doesn't get hit by hurricanes, as it is too far inland. All it receives are occasional rainstorms from hurricane aftermaths. However, Utah does have its own town named Hurricane, in the southwest section of the state. According to the website Utah's Dixie (www.utahsdixie.info):

> *Visitors traveling through Hurricane might wonder why a town in southern Utah shares its name with a tropical cyclone—a type of storm that never has and never will make "landfall" in the inland desert. The curious name dates back to the early 1860s, when a whirlwind blew off the top of a buggy carrying a group of surveyors led by Mormon leader Erastus Snow. "Well, that was a Hurricane," exclaimed Snow. "We'll name this the Hurricane Hill." The nearby fault, mesa, and, later on, the town, took the same moniker. How residents say the name might catch many off guard. Locals pronounce it "Her-ah-kun," which is the British pronunciation.*

That pronunciation is likely because many of the area's early residents emigrated from England. But checking with some present-day emigrants from Britain, they all pronounce the word in the standard way, "hurra-cane." So, British pronunciation has apparently changed over time.

The book *Utah Place Names* by John W. Van Cott gives basically the same origin for the town's name as does Utah's Dixie. Van Cott adds that Snow was the LDS Church leader in charge of its "Dixie" mission to grow cotton.

The Paiute Indians, the first known inhabitants of the Hurricane area, used to call the place Timpoweap, meaning "rock canyon."

11

FIRST ASCENT OF ANGELS LANDING

Angels Landing is defined by Zion National Park as one of its strenuous hikes. It is five and four-tenths miles roundtrip and climbs a total of 1,488 feet. "Not for young children," according to the National Park Service, the final mile of the hike is dominated by sheer vertical cliffs and drop-offs. This trail is not for the faint of heart or for those afraid of heights. In fact, metal chains were added decades ago for additional safety, providing something solid that hikers can hold on to. Many steps have also been cut into the rocks.

The *Washington County News* of December 25, 1924, contained what might be the first recorded climb up Angels Landing. Others likely climbed it before, but this was possibly the first one publicly recorded. Climbs no doubt were undertaken before there were chains to grab on to and prior to safety improvements.

The story reported that Ranger Harold Russell was believed to be the first to stand on the Angels Landing summit in 1923. Russell was also a guide, along with David Dennett, on this climb reported in the St. George, Utah newspaper.

The climb up and through Refrigerator Canyon was not described as harsh. Pretty much only a fifteen-degree lower temperature than the surrounding area was reported in the narrow canyon by the hiking group. Today, much of the lower Angels Landing trail is paved, but back then, white sand dominated much of it.

The Checkerboard Mesa, on the eastern side of Zion National Park, is an iconic formation in the area. *Author photo.*

There were also no Walter's Wiggle switchbacks, located above Refrigerator Canyon, in 1924—they had not yet been built. Some of the hiking party dangled from ropes in thin air to reach the summit.

Frederick Vining Fisher, an Ogden resident and former pastor of the First Methodist Episcopal Church of Ogden, named Angels Landing and two other Zion Canyon landmarks during a visit there, probably in 1916.

Here's the St. George newspaper report by R.B. Gray on the climb past Scout Lookout to Angels Landing. It was originally published in *Union Pacific* magazine. Note that the archive copy is difficult to read. It has been transcribed as accurately as possible. At a digital newspaper site, the article appears garbled, and much of the left margin is cut off.

> *The crest of the ridge, as it lay before us, first descended to a rugged point, then swept up in a great craggy…curve to the haunt of the Angels; the summit, in fact, appeared lofty and inaccessible that the legend of the angels seemed wholly credible and some of us timidly deliberated the possibilities of joining their ranks. It is relatively easy going down to the gap; beyond that point the ridge narrowed from ten feet to ten inches.*
>
> *It became dizzily steep, and occasionally presented little cliffs of thirty or forty feet that required slow and careful progression by means of ten fingers,*

Angels Landing in Zion National Park was first climbed in 1923. Today, it continues to be regularly conquered, despite steep, dizzying drop-offs. *Liz Arave Hafen photo.*

A large group of hikers enjoy the summit of Angels Landing in an April 2014 picture. The taller Great White Throne sits across from Angels Landing. *Roger Arave photo.*

and prayerful exclamations, assisted by the abdominal muscles. All of the arts of crawling…were imitated. But there were places too steep for all but experts in rock work. A helping hand would clutch an inch thick ledge, put a bit of weight on it and find the friable sandstone as soft as a pie crust; A flat slab grasped…had an exasperating habit of falling down on one's head. There were five hazardous stretches which the guides and several experienced climbers of the mountain scaled unassisted; but the remainder of the party required the aid of ropes let down by these pioneers anchored to their bodies. At some interesting spots the climber dangled over some 1,600 feet of pure mountain air and all of them seemed not displeased when their feet rested again in level rock.

The apex of the monolith broadens out to a sloping platform of some twenty feet at its widest and one hundred feet long, capped by a pogoda-like cone. There a cairn of stones was erected, a scroll of names placed therein, and to its top was fastened the skull of a steer brought from the Tinted Desert north of the Kaibab Forest. Angels Landing projects far into Zion Canyon and tho panoramas from its peak are of the highest grandeur, immediately below us was the Great Organ; opposite in the east, the stupendous mass of The Great White Throne, soaring 1,200 feet higher.

Northward we looked into the dizzy walled red amphitheatre called the Temple of Sinawava and beyond to the Narrows where the ethereal white cone of the Mountain of Mystery rises above the gory precipices. Behind us loomed the majestic, reposeful white cliffs of the upper rim.

Southward, the vision included the entire sweep of the east wall Red Arch Mountain, the Mountain-of-the Sun and the Twin Brothers, glowing in the sun.

Such visits are part of the enduring enchantment of Zion; its magnificent, sculptured masses, displaying all the tones of red from peach blossom pink to the deepest carmine known to lipsticks, and onward through Indian lake and maroon to reds that the shadows turn black; its atmospheric moods of bulk and color; its infinite variety; its unlimited opportunities for pioneer exploration with the reward of matchless vistas of scenes never beheld before by civilized man.

Those of the artistic temperament who seek scenic effects not to be had elsewhere on earth will find Zion satisfactory. It is said that a safe trail may be made at small cost to the spot where the angels land and this will probably be done by next season. The splendid vermillion butte will then become a favored observation point for Zion's increasing throng of visitors.

12

FIRST RECORDED ZION
NARROWS TREKS

The Narrows in Zion National Park are undoubtedly one of the premier hikes in all of Utah. Unique, stupendous and awe-inspiring are among the descriptions applied to the site.

But who were the first to hike the Narrows? Native Americans generally avoided the upper portion of Zion Canyon, as it is dark and narrow—an almost devilish place to them.

Geologist Grove Karl Gilbert was the first man known to traverse the Zion Narrows in 1872 as part of a government survey expedition led by Major John Wesley Powell. Gilbert actually made the trip on horseback. It is believed that he first used the term *the Narrows*.

The origin of the name for the Virgin River, which created the Narrows, is uncertain. The word *virgin* is likely of Spanish origin, in honor of the Virgin Mary. But some records claim that Thomas Virgin, an 1820s explorer and mountain man, is the source of the name.

The river had three other names in the nineteenth century or before. Jedediah Smith named it the Adams River, in honor of U.S. president John Adams. Powell named the river's two forks the Parunuweap and the Mukuntuweap, of Native American origins. Neither of those names stuck. The early Spanairds called it El Rio de Sulfuereo, after nearby hot sulfur springs.

After Gilbert's horseback ride, the Zion Narrows had no known explorers, likely because nearby settlers were tired of the Virgin River periodically flooding its banks, and hiking recreation was still something few had time for amid a harsh western lifestyle.

The Virgin River Narrows in Zion National Park offers unique slot canyon scenery but poses deadly hazards during storms. Liz Arave Hafen is shown hiking there. *Steven Arave photo*.

William H. Flanigan, a Cedar City resident, became a popular explorer of southern Utah. He first hiked the Narrows in June 1900 at age twenty-three, going the entire length from the northeast to Springdale in a single day. (Later, he and a brother, Dave, became known for establishing the cable on Cable Mountain in Zion.)

Horseback trips through the Narrows were fairly common over the decades but were officially banned in the 1960s.

Flanigan told the *Iron County Register* on August 29, 1913, about the Narrows. He then recommended travel by foot. "The entire distance would be through a stream of water from a few inches to two or three feet in depth, in a few places. At some points the canyon partakes of the nature of a tunnel, owing to its winding course and the overhanging ledges above. At no point is the canyon more than 100 yards in width and in many places it is little more than a crevice in the solid rock." Walls of rock rose three thousand feet heavenward, and a narrow canyon ran twelve miles in length.

By 1909, the area had been designated a national monument. It then became Zion National Park in 1919, and visitors began to flocking there. "Upper Zion Has Greatest Thrill, Declares Party" stated the August 24, 1925 *Salt Lake Telegram*. Thirteen men spent two days exploring the Zion Narrows. "Never could one see more than a few hundred yards ahead," the article stated. "The most notable discovery of the trip was the comparative ease at which the course can be presently traveled. Excepting for log jams, which might be easily dispensed with, the journey could be made on horseback," the report continued. "Those making the trip declare that Upper Zion Canyon holds thrills for the tourist not dreamed of."

The next big development at the Zion Narrows was the opening of a formal "Gateway to the Narrows" trail in August 1929. According to the *Iron County Record* of August 21, 1929, the trail was five feet wide and covered with tar and pea gravel. "It eliminates the old narrow sand path and does away with the great many sharp pitches and hard climbs, enabling the tourists more easily to go to the upper reaches of the canyon."

Another item of note was the organization of a Zion Narrows Club in 1941. The *Iron County Record* of September 25, 1941, stated that it was William Flanigan himself who was named "Chief Scout" of this group of twenty men. The new group was planning a big hike through the Narrows in the summer of 1942, but the outbreak of World War II might have impacted that plan.

What apparently no one calculated was the tremendous flood danger to hikers in the Zion Narrows. A storm could happen dozens of miles away

A look down the upper portion of Zion Canyon, possibly in the 1930s, just south of the Zion Narrows. *Courtesy of Utah State Historical Society.*

and out of sight of Zion Park and still flood the canyon. Sheer luck seemed to prevent such a tragedy for decades—that is, until September 1961, when four Murray, Utah Boy Scouts were killed in a flash flood there. Two of the boys' bodies were never found. After that, the National Park Service began to take extra precautions and issue flash-flood warnings.

The next development came in September 1965, when a prominent side canyon of the Zion Narrows, Orderville Gulch, was first hiked. Three Leigh brothers—Ralph, Edwin and Douglas—made what might be the first hike through that narrow canyon into the Zion Narrows. They had to lower themselves over six waterfalls.

Another milestone in the Narrows was completed in 1974, when Otto Fife, then seventy-four, of Cedar City completed his fiftieth trip through the Zion Narrows. He had made his first trek in 1925 at age twenty-five. Among Fife's experiences were the following: He gave a bored Boy Scout a stick and told him to make a notch in it every time they had to cross the river. The boy ended up making 252 notches in a trek along the entire length of the Narrows. In the summer of 1965, Fife was detained two days on high ground in the Narrows because of high water and flash floods. And in 1967, he saw an ill sixty-year-old woman helicoptered out of the Narrows.

13

FIRST TO CONQUER TWIN PEAKS

W hile the American Fork Twin Peaks (above Snowbird ski resort) comprise the two tallest points in Salt Lake County, at 11,489 and 11,433 feet above sea level, respectively, it is the "Broad Forks" version (some 159 feet shorter) that gained the most attention from hikers and climbers during Utah's earliest decades. (Likely, the Broad Fork Twin Peaks appeared to be the tallest summits in the area and thus were the supreme challenge of the day. That's because they were more easily spotted in the valley below.)

The *Deseret News* of November 5, 1897, reported that the Broad Fork version of the Twin Peaks were first climbed in the summer of 1847 by Elder John Brown on August 21, in company with Albert Carrington, Dr. William Rust and a Brother Wilson. The men had camped at the mouth of Big Cottonwood Canyon. At eight o'clock the next morning, they left their horses and, according to Brown's own account: "After toiling about eight hours and being very much fatigued, three of us reached the summit of the west peak." (The fourth party member, Dr. Rust, gave out and stopped by a snowbank high up the mountain.)

The group made some readings and estimated the elevation to be 11,219 feet above sea level. The temperature on top was 55 degrees, as opposed to the 101 in downtown Salt Lake that day. They descended at 5:30 p.m. but got caught in the darkness, but not before they rejoined Dr. Rust.

As we had expected to get back to camp about the middle of the afternoon, we were unprovided with bedding, coats or any kind of arms, wishing to go

Twin Peaks (*center background*) are visible from a sparsely populated Cottonwood Heights area of Salt Lake County in the 1940s. *Courtesy of Utah State Historical Society.*

as lightly loaded as possible, the day before very warm. But, now when the night came, we found it quite cold in the mountains.

While climbing over the rocks, after feeling our way with our hands in order to escape death by falling over a precipice, we became separated and only Brother Carrington and I remained together. At 10 p.m., we laid down under a scrubby tree, being so tired that further progress was impossible and we knew not where the other two men had gone. At length, we found a place between the rocks large enough to lay down. Our bed, however, was by no means horizontal: it had a slope of something like 45 degrees. Instead of feathers, we had pebbles for pillows and coarse sands, which were yet warm from the heat of the sun, for bedding: we kept them warm by our bodies during the remainder of the night.

At 5 o'clock the next morning we arose, being somewhat sore and continued our journey down the mountain side. Hungry and faint, having had neither supper or breakfast, we scrambled over the rocks as best we could.

They met up with Dr. Rust partway down. "We reached our camp at 7:30 a.m., where we found our other companion, who had made his way in at 10 o'clock the night previous. We then returned to the city, satisfied with our first attempt at climbing mountains."

The story reported that only a few men had attempted to climb the peaks between then, 1847, and fifty years later, in 1897. Dr. J.R. Park was one of these climbers. "The Twin Peaks. Three Gentlemen make the ascent to the summits" was an August 22, 1883 headline in the *Deseret News*. Joseph T. Kingsbury and Orson Howard were reported as making a climb of these "Twins."

This 1883 climbing report stated that the climbers started at 5:00 a.m. near Little Cottonwood Canyon, looking for a feasible route to take. They ended up in some "fearfully rugged" terrain and had to scramble upward. They were determined to reach the summits, which they did after eight hours of effort. The men reported the summits as entirely devoid of vegetation, though there was still some snow to deal with. They returned to the valley by 7:00 p.m., making for a fourteen-hour trek. The story estimated the peaks to be 11,060 feet above sea level. (The actual altitudes of these Twin Peaks are 11,328 feet.)

Some three years later, in August 1886, the *Salt Lake Democrat* contained the account of how another two men climbed the Broad Fork Twin Peaks. They rode horses much of the way, leaving their animals in a meadow when the climb became rugged. The men reported a narrow, foot-wide precipice to negotiate with hundred-foot cliffs below. There was also lots of deep snow in the upper areas.

The *Salt Lake Herald* of November 3, 1897, reported on a $100 bet to climb the supposedly previously unclimbed north of the Broad Fork Twin Peaks. Conditions of the bet where that the two men, Herman Neipage and Claud Victor, would leave Murray at sunrise and had to return by sunset after having climbed the summit.

It was reported to be a hard and dangerous climb, with two thousand feet of ledges. Neipage was described as a daring leaper, while Victor used a sixty-foot rope for help. Six hours after sunrise, Victor planted an American flag on the summit and even built a fire just below the summit to show they had made it. They were back in Murray one hour before sunset to collect their $100.

The *Salt Lake Telegram* of July 30, 1912, reported that a group of Salt Lake men scaled the Twin Peaks in just five hours from a base camp in Big Cottonwood Canyon. This was considered a record. The men even took a bulldog along, which had to be lifted over some rocks.

"Local Girls Climb Dizzy Twin Peaks" declared the August 8, 1919 *Salt Lake Herald*. A group of ten females climbed the peaks, led by J.T. Griffiths, physical instructor at the University of Utah. The girls made the hike in twelve hours and without a single drink, as there was no water on the mountainside, it being a dry year.

By 1922, the University of Utah was sponsoring an annual hike to Twin Peaks, according to the *Salt Lake Telegram*. That year was the fifth annual such event. At least twenty-five persons were registered to go that time.

14

FIRSTS IN UTAH SPORTS

After some extensive searches in nineteenth-century Utah newspapers, it was determined that the first baseball game reported as being played in Utah Territory was on July 24, 1871. The paper stated that the Salt Lake Twentieth Ward of the LDS Church played that first contest—at least the first one reported by a local newspaper. The ward's "Star" baseball club played a contest, and the prize was a "handsome bat and ball."

The ward also staged some running races and jumping contests on the holiday commemorating the Mormon pioneers' arrival into the Salt Lake Valley on July 24, 1847.

The first Utah Territory reference to the sport of bowling was in the *Salt Lake Tribune* of December 18, 1871. The report stated that the Pioneer Bowling Alley had reduced the cost of a ten-pin game to twenty-five cents. (Obviously, since the bowling alley was already there, the sport had been played in Salt Lake City since at least earlier that year.)

The *Salt Lake Herald* of May 24, 1885, contained what may be the first reference to tennis in Utah. The newspaper stated that a lawn tennis competition between Murdock and Hull of Zion's Co-operative Mercantile Institution (ZCMI) and Roberts and Eccles ended in a tie after four sets. "Another game will probably be played shortly," the *Herald* stated.

The *Salt Lake Tribune* reported on May 21, 1880, that the first known game of "foot Ball" had been played on the Eight Ward's Square between the Olympic and the St. Mark's teams. No score was reported.

"University Basket-Ball. Girls Defeat the Boys in the First Open Game" was a May 16, 1897 headline in the *Salt Lake Tribune*. The story reported that in the premiere game played on the new outdoor field at the University of Utah, the women's squad beat the men's team by a score of 8–6. Thus, women not only played the first recorded game of hoops in Utah but also defeated the men.

The beginnings of the sport of golf in Utah were probably more social than athletic. In fact, the headline for one of the first golf stories in a Utah newspaper stated: "Salt Lake's smart set opens golf season at the county club's links. The affair takes the form of a social function more than an athletic event." The *Salt Lake Telegram* of April 5, 1902, stated this was the third annual event, meaning organized golf first took off in Utah in 1899.

The *Telegram* story continued: "Club members as a rule wore the regulation golf dress, the women in scarlet coats, short shirts and golf shoes, the men in similar coats, loud checked knickerbockers and golf shoes, while of the invited guests the women gave an excellent display of the spring fashions and the men conformed for the most part to the dictates of fashion in frock coat and silk hat."

An earlier golf story, this one in the April 22, 1900 edition of the *Salt Lake Tribune*, reported: "Golf tournament is opened. First match played yesterday on the grounds of the Country Club, thirteen members playing" (This country club was on Eleventh East Street.)

Such was the beginnings of Utah golf. In the early years, other reports indicated that the sport was too exclusive and expensive for the average person.

Almost six decades before the first *Deseret News* Marathon (26.2 miles, in 1970), there was the first public "marathon" footrace in Salt Lake City. Sponsored by the Commercial Club of Salt Lake, it was promoted by local newspapers as a marathon, while race organizers referred to it as a "cross-city run." The *Salt Lake Herald* of November 4, 1913, billed it as the first modified marathon to be held in the state.

According to the *Salt Lake Tribune* of December 7, 1913, this was a 5.0-mile race. (Although that's 21.2 miles short of today's official marathon distance, the farthest distance University of Utah cross-country runners raced that year was 3.0 miles, according to the *Telegram* of October 29, 1913.)

"Williams Wins Marathon; Race Is Great Success," was the *Tribune*'s headline after the first "marathon." Herbert N. Williams of Salt Lake grabbed first place in a time of 29:31.8 (or just under 6:00 per mile). Williams was in the lead from the start and was never challenged. Forty-five men started the

The University of Utah women's basketball team ("Basketeers") made history, as illustrated in this *Salt Lake Tribune* drawing from April 18, 1897. *Courtesy of Salt Lake Tribune Archives.*

race, but only twenty-nine finished. In fact, a *Telegram* headline on December 4—three days before the race—had stated, "Club May Abandon Proposed Run across City," due to a lack of entrants.

The race was held at 4:00 p.m. on Saturday, December 6—oddly, a wintertime race, though photographs show most runners wearing shorts. (Fortunately, there was no snow on the ground.) Organizers apparently chose that time of year for a race because similar races were regularly held in eastern states in late fall. Orin Jackson, a Brigham Young College of Logan runner, fainted at the finish line but quickly recovered.

Yet the race was more of an obstacle course than how road races are staged today. "Every conceivable annoyance was put in the way of the runners," the *Tribune* story stated. "Although the Commercial Club field sports committee had done everything within its power to keep the course clear, the road was packed with automobiles and vehicles of all sorts, to say nothing of hundreds of men, boys and dogs. It is a fact that Williams and those who finished immediately after him had to fight their way through a dense crowd before they could touch the finishing line."

There was also a street-paving job underway at Ninth South and State Streets that runners had to maneuver through. Some runners also had to run off the road through weeds and embankments to get past heavy auto traffic. "A couple of the entrants took advantage of passing autos 'to get a lift.' The inspectors of the course, however quickly spotted them." The race started and ended at the Pioneer Monument at South Temple and Main Streets.

The historic race saw other controversies. Autos measured the course at five and two-tenths miles, not five miles. Also, the *Telegram*'s race results story of December 6 stated that Williams won the race by a full city block. But the newspaper stated on December 8 that the end of the race course was so blocked with automobiles that no other runner could have passed Williams had they possessed the endurance to do so.

The *Salt Lake Telegram* of December 4, 1913, stated, "Commercial Club Is Too Generous with Its Marathon Prizes." That's because a $200 motorcycle went to the winner (more than $5,000 in 2023 terms). The Amateur Athletic Union (AAU) at the time had a rule that any prizes over $50 made a runner a professional, according to the story. Some runners, particularly prep and collegiate runners, worried that winning such a prize would affect their amateur status.

"Keen Interest in Long Distance Runs," declared the *Telegram* on November 22, 1913, before the race, illustrating a national and local trend in the rising popularity of footraces. All Utah colleges then, except BYU in Logan, sponsored cross-country races. High schools were considering doing the same. (Previously, bicycle competitions—often by professionals—had been the racing rage in Utah for decades.)

The sequel to that first Salt Lake marathon was a high-school-only version that next spring. According to the *Tribune* of March 21, 1914, Munn Cannon of Salt Lake High School (today's West High) won that two-and-one-quarter-mile race in 14:17. Medals, not prizes were awarded to the top finishers.

Less than a year after the Commercial Club's inaugural race, the Deseret Gymnasium organized a second "cross-city" race on October 21, 1916. The prizes for this race were well publicized. According to the *Salt Lake Tribune* of October 9, the top two finishers received an expense-paid trip to Denver to compete in a race there. The third-place finisher received a gold watch, the fourth-place finisher received a sweater coat and the fifth-place racer won a jewelry box.

15

TRANSPORTATION FIRSTS IN UTAH

The very first automobile was spotted in Salt Lake City on April 12, 1899. "First Horseless Carriage Seen on Salt Lake Streets," was the headline in the April 13, 1899 *Salt Lake Herald*.

That first machine of its kind in Salt Lake was a Winton Motor Carriage and sold for $1,500 (more than $37,000 in 2023 terms). The newspaper report stated that the auto attracted "much attention" as it traveled along Main Street, State Street and West Temple Street. It seemed to especially delight young boys in town, who lined up along the road to watch it.

The Salt Lake Hardware Company bought the horseless carriage and transported it to Salt Lake from Cleveland, Ohio, with the help of George E. Aris, son of a well-known Utah miner.

By 1906, autos were much more common on Salt Lake City streets. But traffic control was an increasing concern, as was "fast driving," the earliest term for speeding.

It may not have been the first airplane sighting in Utah, but it was early enough to cause quite a stir among residents. On October 13, 1919, the *Standard-Examiner* stated, "One of Racing Airplanes Passes over Ogden, Causing a Craning of Many Necks." Major Harry Smith flew his gray plane over Ogden that morning on his transcontinental trip, which would also fly over Salt Lake City and eventually reach San Francisco. Smith was the first to fly a route along the Union Pacific Railroad tracks. He exited Weber Canyon and then veered northwest into Ogden at about 115 miles per hour.

A newspaper illustration of the first automobile—"Horseless carriage"—driving through Salt Lake City on April 12, 1899. *Courtesy of Salt Lake Herald.*

Most residents heard the "whirr" of the airplane's motor long before they spotted it and were delighted at the sight. "Flying to Salt Lake in twenty-one minutes is a big deal and his mark will no doubt stand for some time," the *Standard* reported.

III

Gone but Not Forgotten

16

GREAT SALT LAKE'S
VANISHED RESORTS

Mormon pioneers and early settlers were fanatically attracted to the Great Salt Lake, a vast salty body of water with no outlet where bathers could "float like a cork." About ten accommodations sprouted up by the late 1800s. None survive today as formal resorts at their original locations.

The lake's fickle habit of greatly shrinking and then enlarging again played havoc on the beachfronts of the resorts over the years. The public also soon favored freshwater swimming or hot springs over a briny experience.

And the popularity of the automobile meant that Utahns could drive to the mountains and out of state—basically, to places not rigidly set by railroad travel only. (Most Great Salt Lake resorts had railroad access and were even created to drive passenger traffic to the rails.)

One confusing element of the former Great Salt Lake resorts was the overuse of the term *lake* in resort titles. This led to plenty of historical confusion over the years; some resorts had their histories incorrectly mixed up with other resorts. For example, Lake Side in Kaysville is sometimes confused with Lake Park in Farmington. The history book *Layton, Utah* by the Kaysville-Layton Historical Society somehow managed to confuse Lake Side with Lake Park. This is significant, because Lake Park eventually moved eastward and became Lagoon Amusement Park, the largest such establishment in the Intermountain West. Note also that the Lake Shore resort is also sometimes confused with the Syracuse resort.

This 1897 photograph by T.D. Rust captures a quieter view of Garfield Beach resort's promenade and pavilion four years after rival Saltair opened nearby. *Courtesy of Library of Congress*.

One big void in the ten lake resorts' geography was a lack of any lake resort that Ogden—Utah's second-largest city at the time—could lay claim to. The city had plans for such a resort to be built in the Promontory Point / Little Mountain area, directly west of today's Twelfth Street in Ogden. But that dream never became a reality, though it was promoted heavily from 1912 to 1923.

What follows are some historical glances at eight of the most popular Great Salt Lake resorts of yesteryear.

Lake Side was located southwest of Kaysville (but close to the Farmington border) and opened in June 1870. It was probably the first

"Floating like a cork" was a popular summer pastime for northern Utahns and visitors at the turn of the twentieth century. *Courtesy of Library of Congress.*

standard attraction along the lake's shore. It monopolized the resort trade for several years, with numerous church and family outings. John W. Young, third son of Brigham Young, built it. This Young had part ownership in the Utah Central Railroad.

A key highlight of the resort was that it eventually featured a twenty-five-cent ride on the *City of Corinne*, a steamboat, going to Lake Point on the south shore. This former commercial ship on the lake took tourists during the 1872 season on excursions. The boat could carry one hundred passengers and even boasted its own live band. In the 1882 season, Lake Side provided some thirty thousand "baths" in the Great Salt Lake.

It is unclear exactly when this resort vanished, but it's certain that the low lake level of the early 1890s would have closed it. And the popularity of the much larger Lake Park, which opened to the south sixteen years later, in 1886, also likely killed it.

Lake Point was started in 1870, about the same time as Lake Side. It was built by Dr. Jeter Clinton and offered sandy beaches. By 1874, it had a dining hall and a dancing room, plus forty hotel rooms. On July 4, 1876, some 1,500 people visited the resort.

Today's Lake Point Junction, along I-80, is the only ghost left of the resort. It likely fell victim to Saltair's popularity by or before 1890.

Black Rock was opened by H.J. Faust in 1876, but this resort didn't catch on, either. It soon fell into disrepair, something quickly possible along the lake's shores, given the corrosive salt water, winds and storms.

Alonzo Hyde, son-in-law of LDS Church president John Taylor, and David John Taylor, the president's son, took over Black Rock in 1880. It was located a few miles northeast of Lake Point. The resort was named for the large black rock monolith that's in or along the lake, depending on its level.

Heber C. Kimball's old ranch house was turned into a hotel, and the resort had swings and a merry-go-round pulled by a horse. But a much larger and grander resort, Saltair, opened in 1893 and put Black Rock out of business by the mid-1890s.

Black Rock was resurrected in 1933, but that didn't last. (Sunset Beach in 1934 was still another small resort that operated for a short time on the lake's south shore, but it couldn't compete with Saltair. Today, it "survives" as just a beach area with no accessories.)

Lake Shore was described as a modest little resort. It opened in 1879 and was located a few miles southwest of where Lake Park (Lagoon's forerunner) would be. George O. Chase was one of the owners.

Like Lake Side, little is known about Lake Shore. It had some dressing rooms, but that apparently was it. Lake Shore was described as being fifteen miles north of Salt Lake City and reached by the Central Railroad system.

Again, the establishment of the larger Lake Park in 1886 and the receding lake level would have doomed Lake Shore by 1890 or sooner.

Garfield Beach began in 1881 and was located two miles southwest of Black Rock. It capitalized on service via the steamboat from Lake Side. The boat was renamed *General Garfield*, in honor of James A. Garfield having taken a ride on it. The boat was anchored semipermanently offshore of the resort.

In 1887, the Garfield resort was purchased by the Utah and Nevada Railroad. Some $100,000 in improvements were added, including two hundred bathhouses with showers, a restaurant, a racetrack and a bowling alley. It was then called "Utah's great sanitarium resort," and eighty-four thousand people visited Garfield that year.

Five years later, it was still going strong, and the Union Pacific Railroad purchased it and spent another $150,000 in upgrades. It was the lake's first resort to have an electric generator and lights. A fire destroyed the resort and the steamboat in 1904. Despite rumors that the resort would be rebuilt, it never was.

Lake Park started on July 15, 1886, between Lake Side and Lake Shore. Railroad magnate Simon Bamberger (later Utah's first Democratic governor) built the resort with a $100,000 investment as a proven way to increase passenger traffic on his trains. It was promoted as one of the "most attractive watering places in the West." Some 53,000 people visited Lake Park in its first season.

Based on 1886 lake levels, it was probably located one and seven-tenths miles west of today's Lagoon. It boasted an open-air dancing pavilion, a small Victorian-style hotel and a string of cabanas along the beach—some 120 acres in all. A sailboat racing and rowing club also had headquarters at Lake Park.

By 1895, the resort was suffering from low water levels. What once was lakeshore was now blue-colored mud. Guests had to walk a third of a mile or more to reach the water. Bamberger decided to move the resort inland to a swampy area. Five of the resort's original buildings were moved. The park reopened as Lagoon on July 12, 1896. The relocation, away from fickle lake levels to another lake—a small, freshwater one—proved wise. The result is today's Lagoon, the largest amusement park between the Midwest and California.

Syracuse Resort opened on July 4, 1887, when thirteen train cars of bathers and a total of two thousand people turned out. A train line from Ogden ended at the ninety-three-acre resort. The resort was built by Daniel C. Adams and Fred Kiesel where today's causeway to Antelope Island begins along 1700 South, west of the Syracuse city limits.

It was described as "an oasis in the desert." Unique among lake resorts, it had a grove of trees transplanted from Weber Canyon. Boat excursions were offered to nearby lake islands. It had seventy bathhouses. A picnic area in the shade of the trees was four hundred yards from the lakeshore. That area was also used for outdoor LDS Church conferences in the area. A horse-driven streetcar traveled between the picnic area and bathhouses.

Syracuse Resort even staged bicycle races on a nearby dirt track. Artesian wells and water tanks served the resort. It had a dance pavilion suspended on pilings, but later, some pilings slipped, and the dance floor warped.

Trains were known to sometimes strand people at the resort. For example, on July 8, 1889, a group from Ogden had to spend the night there when the night's only train left early.

Syracuse Resort closed in 1892 from a twofold problem: a dispute over ownership of the land and the receding waters of the lake that left it mired in mud. Area industries used the railroad tracks for some decades, but they have been long since removed, and no trace of the old resort is to be found today.

Saltair, the lake's last legendary resort, was also its most elegant and popular. Only it was grand enough to have the magic to survive past the early 1900s. It opened on Memorial Day 1893 at a cost of $350,000. It was built over the lake itself on 2,500 ten-inch wooden pilings. It originally had 1,000 bathhouses and was started and owned by the Church of Jesus Christ of Latter-day Saints.

Saltair's turreted pavilion rises like a royal palace above the Great Salt Lake in a 1901 photograph. It was located about sixteen miles from Salt Lake City. *Courtesy of the Library of Congress.*

Some ten thousand people came out for its official dedication on June 8, 1893. Its main hall was similar in size and shape to the Mormon Tabernacle. It boasted a fifty-cent train ride from Salt Lake; the ticket included Saltair admission.

Saltair eventually became a world-class resort and wanted to be the "Coney Island of the West." In the early 1900s, it was a popular place for church groups, though the resort struggled with whether or not to sell alcohol on-site. By 1906, the resort had been sold to a group of private investors. Its overall annual attendance went from 250,000 in 1906 to 450,000 in 1919.

The resort seemed a magnet for natural disasters. Two windstorms in 1910 destroyed two hundred bathhouses and other structures. A large fire in 1925 caused $500,000 damage, with insurance covering only $100,000. But two and half months after the fire, Saltair was open again. Another fire struck in 1931, damaging its coaster and amusement rides. By then, Saltair had a tunnel of love, six bowling alleys, a Ferris wheel, a fish pond, a funhouse, pool halls, a penny arcade, a photo gallery, a shooting gallery and a roller-skating rink. It was described as the "biggest amusement value in the world" in the 1930s.

Saltair was also billed as having the world's largest dance floor, where five thousand people could foxtrot at once in the open-air hall. But Saltair continued to be plagued by disasters. In 1932, a windstorm killed two construction workers. In 1939, a fire destroyed its pier.

The resort closed from 1944 to 1945, during World War II, because of gas rationing and other problems. Yet another fire damaged it in 1955 and destroyed many bathhouses. A freak wind gust destroyed its roller coaster in 1957. By 1959, the State of Utah had taken possession of the crumbling resort and closed it.

The abandoned resort burned to the ground in November 1970. In 1983, Wally Wright spent $3 million to build a new Saltair resort about a mile west of the original site. But within a year, the lake level was rising and the new Saltair was struggling to survive. Saltair III is still there, but only as a specter of the old "Lady of the Lake" that existed there in the early part of the previous century.

NORTHERN UTAH OLD HOT SPRINGS

T hey used to be one of the hottest spots in northern Utah, rivaling the Great Salt Lake resorts.

Once, hordes of swimmers and bathers enjoyed hot-spring resorts. Most of these resorts traced their roots to the pioneer era. In the first half of their twentieth-century heyday, there were at least a dozen such commercial hot springs stretching from Box Elder County to Utah County and from Morgan to Wasatch Counties. Early residents believed the hot, mineral-laden water had healing powers.

Like the GSL resorts, some of the histories of these vanished hot springs are confusing. For example, Becks Hot Spring and Warm (Wasatch) Springs were often confused and even interchanged, being less than a mile apart at the north end of Salt Lake City. Warms Springs, the state's first used hot spot, began about 1849, and Beck Springs started shortly after that.

Today, Warm/Wasatch Springs, which closed in 1976 and was then the Children's Museum building, is now just an unsafe building waiting to be torn down, while remnants of Beck's Hot Springs can often be spotted, with steaming water vapor rising up in winter near I-15's sharp curve at the north end of Salt Lake County.

Also, two "crater/cone" hot springs in Midway, Wasatch County, got confused over the years. Today, the Homestead hot spring survives as the Crater, but it was originally known as Schnietter's Hot Pot in the 1890s. There was also a Luke's Hot Springs in Midway.

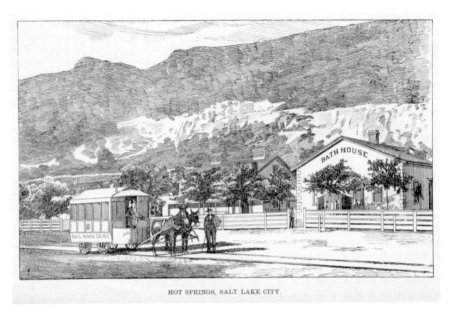

HOT SPRINGS, SALT LAKE CITY.

This is a drawing of the Warm Springs resort (later called Wasatch Springs), probably in the 1870s. *Courtesy of Wikipedia Commons.*

In addition, there used to be Castilla Hot Springs (started in 1889), located about three miles up Spanish Fork Canyon. Today, only a few cement vaults remain. Also, Firth Water Hot Springs is a two-and-three-tenths-mile hike up Diamond Canyon in Spanish Fork Canyon today.

Yet Utah County's supreme hot spring was probably Saratoga Springs, first used in 1854. It closed by the late 1970s and is a housing development now. Still, a mile or so south—and by the edge of Utah Lake—are several Saratoga hot pots that are more like mud pots, though they are still visited by avid users of the Jordan River trail.

Morgan boasted Como Springs for many decades. It began in 1889 and closed to swimming in 1985. Today, it is a camping oasis, though the owner would like to bring back some of the resort's original features.

Weber County had Utah Hot Springs in Pleasant View, right next to the main railroad line. It was used from the 1880s until the early 1970s and had a giant slide in its outdoor pool. Today, the hot, natural water is used by a greenhouse operation.

Rainbow Gardens used to be known as the Ogden Canyon Sanitarium and dates to the 1890s. Then, it was El Monte Springs and Riverside Gardens until 1946, when the Rainbow title took over. Rainbow offered indoor and

Left: Venice Carson Flygare (*center*) enjoys Crystal Hot Springs resort in 1948 with friends Doris and Lee. *Courtesy of Harold Flygare Family photo collection.*

Below: The modern Crystal Hot Springs includes a waterslide and outdoor hot pools in a rural setting in Box Elder County. *Author photo.*

One of the pioneer hot springs craters in Midway, Utah, possibly the Udy Hot Springs area, in the 1880s. *Courtesy of the Library of Congress.*

outdoor pools until 1972. Today, the outdoor pool is in disrepair and the indoor pool is part of a terraced gift garden. The actual hot spring is located about six hundred yards east, up the Ogden River. It is used today despite being on private property, complete with no trespassing signs.

Box Elder County still has Crystal Hot Springs in operation year-round in Honeyville. This resort opened in 1901. It added a waterslide in the late 1980s. Despite being a popular camping area, camping ceased about 2020.

Udy Hot Springs, now called Belmont Springs, is located northwest of Crystal Springs, in Garland. It opened in the 1890s and now offers just a thirty-five-foot-deep pool for scuba diving.

It is also worth noting that there are a few other, lesser-known hot springs in northern Utah. For example, "Stinky Springs" is located near Thiokol, west of Brigham City. It was never developed commercially, and vandals have destroyed its makeshift facilities. Grouse Creek also has at least one warmwater spring.

Cache Valley used to have Loganna in Logan. But by the early 1980s, this waterslide/swimming resort was sold to accommodate a housing project.

One of two popular large outdoor hot pools in Saratoga, along the shores of Utah Lake. The pools are accessible via the Jordan River Parkway. *Author photo*.

This is the large hot pool at Belmont Hot Springs in Garland, Utah. This pool is also sometimes used for scuba-diving training. *Author photo*.

Why do so many hot springs exist in northern Utah? Paul Jewell, associate professor of geology and geophysics at the University of Utah, said the Great Basin is an area where the crust of the Earth is being stretched. That makes the crust thinner and means the mantle of the Earth, a warm layer, is closer to the surface. Water circulates through the crust and is heated at these shallow depths. With some good natural plumbing, these hot springs are usually associated with breaks along segments of the Wasatch Fault.

18

A SWITZERLAND-LIKE TRAM
IN PROVO CANYON

The younger generation may never know the thrill that was the exotic taste of Switzerland in Provo Canyon. For nearly fifty years, a tram line rose sharply to the top of Provo Canyon, passing Bridal Veil Falls and offering incredible views of the area.

Yes, there are other tram lines, like the one at Snowbird in Little Cottonwood Canyon, but this old tramway, the "Sky Ride," was unique. It boasted four superlatives: (1) It was the steepest tram line in the world, rising 1,228 vertical feet in just 1,753 feet of cable. (Some people would not ride it, as it looked so unrealistically steep. Others would crawl out of the tram on top, scared out of their wits.) (2) It was the only tram that sat right next to a major U.S. highway. (3) It was the only U.S. tram that passed by a major waterfall. (4) It was the only U.S. tram that had a river running directly below it and just feet from its starting point.

The Provo Canyon Tram last operated on New Year's Day 1996.

The tram line opened in 1961. Its construction produced one fatality. An equipment worker died after driving a bulldozer over the cliff above the tram during its mid-1960s construction process.

The tram climbed as sharply as sixty-six degrees. During its seasonal operation (May–October), it would carry almost thirty thousand riders a season to the top.

The demise of the tram line was a result of several events. An avalanche greatly damaged the tram's equipment on that fateful New Year's Day. Then, just over two years later, as the owners, the Grow family, were working to

The "Sky Ride" was a popular attraction in Provo Canyon for nearly fifty years, climbing the Wasatch Mountains near Bridal Veil Falls. *Author photo.*

restore the tram, a man-made fire, likely arson, damaged the cable line and other equipment. There used to be a restaurant on top of the tram, later an events venue for weddings, reunions and other celebrations called Eagle's Nest Lodge.

The Grows' reopening of the site was stopped after the January 1, 1996 avalanche by a $100,000 environmental study required by the U.S. Forest Service. The fire struck the next year. Not long after the fire, the Grows had to have the cable lines taken down for safety reasons. So it appeared the flavor of Switzerland in Provo Canyon was over. And a 2007–8 plan to reopen the facility failed.

The Grows, of Orem, had owned the tram resort since 1971. Rue L. Clegg bought the land in 1936 and opened it with the tram in 1961. He died

SKY-RIDE DATA

1. Tramway built in Switzerland. Meets Swiss government regulations.
2. Safety factor of 5. Designed to carry five times full load capacity of gondolas.
3. Telephones in gondolas and at terminals.
4. Distance from lower to top terminal is 1753 feet.
5. Vertical rise 1228 feet. Steepest in the world.
6. Each track cable weighs 1½ tons.
7. Two 14 ton counter-weights (in basement) keep cables taut.
8. Smaller cables pull gondolas up and down on large track cables.
9. Top terminal anchored in limestone with steel and 60 cubic yards of concrete.
10. Tramway operates on "jig-back" system —like buckets in a well.
11. This is the only tramway in the world adjoining a highway, overlooking a river, and passing a waterfall.

Left: The "Sky Ride" tram climbed nearly two thousand vertical feet to a mountaintop resort/restaurant. The tram opened in 1961 and closed permanently in 1996. *Author photo.*

Right: This billboard at the "Sky Ride" billed it as the steepest tram line in the world. The owners hoped to reopen it but failed. *Author photo.*

of a heart attack in 1963, and his wife took over the business before selling it eight years later to the Grows.

The tram weathered many avalanches over the years. For example, in 1983, a record snowfall wiped out the path at the top of the mountain crest leading from the top of the tram to a view westward of Utah County.

Finally, in the spring of 2017, all leftover tram ride materials and mountaintop building materials were torn out in an effort to return the area to its original state. All traces of the attraction are now gone.

TIMPANOGOS PEAK'S ANNUAL BYU HIKE OF OLD

Timpanogos Peak is the second-highest point in the Wasatch Mountain range at 11,750 feet. It is also the most prominent peak in Utah County and is climbed by thousands of people each year. In the past, it became a victim of its own popularity, as an almost six-decade annual mass hike to the summit had to be discontinued.

Eugene L. Roberts, the director of physical education at Brigham Young University, started a new school tradition in July 1912, sponsoring a hike to the "Timp" summit. He led a combined group of twenty-two students and teachers on a three-day expedition to the top of that lofty peak.

Yes, many others had already hiked the Timpanogos summit before that, but it was Roberts who envisioned it as a "Wonder Mountain" that made it more than merely a lofty place. This was a religious place.

The idea for the mass hike came from Roberts's service as a full-time missionary of the Church of Jesus Christ of Latter-day Saints. Serving in Switzerland, he watched some five thousand Catholics in 1908 hike in a religious pilgrimage to worship at a shrine high in the Swiss Alps. In fact, in 1912, it took two wagons pulled by horses for the group of twenty-two to reach the start of their landmark hike in the north fork of Provo Canyon (today's Aspen Grove). The road was rough, and the trip was slow going. "It required nearly eight hours to reach [the summit] since there were no real trails up the mountain side, and much of the distance led through dense underbrush," Roberts said of the original landmark hike in 1912.

A pair of hikers scrambles toward Timpanogos Peak in the 1940s. *Courtesy of Utah State Historical Society*.

An unidentified man on a horse with a packhorse behind is photographed just below the summit of Timpanogos Peak in the summer of 1930. *Courtesy of Utah State Historical Society*.

Indeed, Roberts soon after required the nickname "Timp" because of his passion for the mountain. Today, one of the smaller summits on the backside of Timpanogos Mountain is unofficially often referred to as "Robert's Horn" (10,993 feet high), in honor of the BYU professor.

Professor Roberts later added songs, a campfire program and even fireworks to the annual hiking event. He envisioned a mountain pageant to accompany the hiking event, but that never came to be. "There is no way of predicting [the annual hike's] future, but one thing is sure, it is worthwhile, and has contributed and will continue to contribute much toward the richness of Utah community recreational life," Roberts stated before his passing on July 9, 1953, at the age of seventy-three.

This annual hike became more popular each year, and by the end of the tradition in 1970, the event was attracting thousands of hikers. And that's what killed the tradition: too many hikers on the mountain at once, creating not only unsafe conditions (with rolling boulders and rock) but also ecological damage to the trail and mountain itself. Today, the designated Timpanogos Wilderness Area has a fifteen-person-per-group limit to avoid mistakes of the past.

With an abundance of small waterfalls, blooming flowers and alpine scenery unparalleled in the Beehive State (and more akin to Switzerland), there's no reason to not understand why a Timp hike is so appealing.

In the decades following Roberts's death, some turned the hike into a race, bragging about how quickly they went up and down the mountain. But Roberts had urged hikers to not be in a hurry. "Prepare to remain on the mountain until late afternoon. Many people hurry up and then hurry back. This is a mistake. When going through heaven, take it easy," he said.

20

THE SHORT-LIVED YEARLY TREK
TO MOUNT NEBO

Mount Nebo, the highest pinnacle in the Wasatch Mountains, at 11,928 feet above sea level, had its own annual mass hiking event. After all, Nebo was taller than Timpanogos Peak, and Juab County was not to be outdone by neighboring Utah County and its annual "Timp" hike. "Aloft on Mount Nebo; Utah Peak Has Beauty of Alps; Grandeur in View," was a March 1, 1920 headline in the *Salt Lake Herald*.

By then, a "safe trail" to the summit had been made from Salt Creek, also today's most-used path. This path was constructed in 1919, and some eighty-two people climbed to its summit on August 6, 1919, the start of an annual mass group pilgrimage to Mount Nebo. An estimated three thousand people in the summer of 1919 enjoyed camping on the back side of Mount Nebo in the Salt Creek area.

The *Manti Messenger* of July 31, 1925, reported that the Kiwanis Club of Nephi was a sponsor of an annual hike up Mount Nebo. It was held on August 5 that year, under a full moon, so that hikers could enjoy the sunrise at the summit. That Salt Creek trail to Mount Nebo was referred to as the "trail of a thousand turns." The story also referred to Nebo as a "solitary sentinel of the southern Wasatch."

By 1927, the annual hike was still being held on the night of a full moon, August 12 that year, complete with a bonfire and full festival at the Salt Creek camping area. The only concerns reported were for proper sanitation and fire hazards.

This aerial photograph from 1945 shows the east side of Mount Nebo, the highest peak in the Wasatch Range. *Courtesy of Utah State Historical Society.*

This August 1994 photograph shows Ray Boren on the south summit of Mount Nebo. The mountain clearly has three separate pinnacles. *Ravell Call photo.*

The annual hike up Mount Nebo probably continued for some years after. It likely died out for some of the same reasons that eventually doomed the much more popular annual summer hike up Mount Timpanogos: too many people on the mountain at once for proper safety and conservation.

Also, unlike Timp Peak, the trail to Mount Nebo lacks any streams or waterfalls. Although the view on top of Nebo was second to none in the Wasatch, the trail to get there was simply not as enticing as the one to Timp. In addition, the Nebo hike lacked the support of a major university like BYU, and Juab County's population was sparse compared to that of Utah County, and it also lacked a more populated county on its eastern side, like Timp has with Wasatch County.

21

UTAH'S FORMER
"TEMPLES OF HEALTH"

O ne of the most exciting developments in Salt Lake City during the early twentieth century was the opening of the Deseret Gymnasium in 1910. This "Temple of Health," as some referred to it, existed for some eighty-seven years. (It also served many non–LDS Church members in the area.)

Not to be outdone, Ogden residents lobbied for their own Deseret Gymnasium, and it opened in 1925 (decades before Ogden had its own spiritual temple).

Salt Lake's Deseret Gymnasium opened its doors on September 20, 1910. Located where the LDS Church Office Building now stands on North Temple Street, the gym was just east of the Salt Lake Temple. It was part of the old downtown LDS University and used by students and the public. Its official grand opening featured an orchestra. The facility cost $250,000 (more than $6.14 million in 2023 terms).

The centerpiece of the gym was its thirty-by-sixty-foot swimming pool. Indeed, the *Salt Lake Telegram* stated on September 17, 1910, that an early opening of just the pool proved to be a chaotic and unpredictable affair. "A mob of more than a thousand attacked the Deseret gymnasium at the rear of the Latter-day Saints' University this morning and for a time it looked as though the doors would be battered down and the building would be taken by a storm."

The gym had advertised that any boy age seven and up would be admitted free that morning, hence the mob. "An average of 100 boys an hour were

The Deseret Gymnasium construction takes shape in 1909 in downtown Salt Lake City, near the Salt Lake Temple. *Courtesy of Utah State Historical Society*.

The Deseret Gymnasium / First Weber State College Gymnasium in Ogden was a popular hub promoting physical fitness for many decades. *Author photo*.

admitted to the pool," the story stated. Some 1,500 boys got a free swim that day. The pool was four and a half to eight and a half feet deep.

Men and women had separate hours of pool usage during the gym's early decades. The original gym also contained six bowling alleys, a basketball court and much more.

In April 1911, the Deseret Gymnasium had athletes put on exhibitions for General Conference visitors, with calisthenics, folk dancing and games, according to the *Salt Lake Tribune* of April 5, 1911. On March 9, the paper stated that indoor baseball games had been held inside the Deseret Gym.

In the early 1960s, the Salt Lake Deseret Gym was aging and deemed too small. A new, larger gym was built to the northwest and opened in 1965. It featured a much larger swimming pool and an indoor track above its main basketball court.

There was also a popular barbershop in the building, and many a departing missionary for the LDS Church had their hair cut there in the 1960s and early 1970s, before the Missionary Training Center came along in Provo.

The Salt Lake Deseret Gymnasium closed in 1997 to make way for the new Conference Center a block north of Temple Square. Ogden's Deseret Gymnasium, 550 Twenty-Fifth Street, closed in the early 1990s and was sold in 1993 to Total Fitness.

Today, such gymnasiums are probably not needed, at least ones operated by the LDS Church, since many private gym/fitness and swimming facilities now exist.

22

ANDERSON TOWER

Short-Lived Salt Lake Attraction

Mention Anderson Tower, and few Salt Lake City residents will have any idea what you are talking about. That's because this lofty granite landmark has been gone for approximately a century (so almost no person alive will recall having viewed it), and it existed for only forty-eight total years anyway. Today, all that remains of the tower is a monument near its original location at about 303 "C" Street.

This tower was built by Robert R. Anderson of Salt Lake City in 1886 of granite, from the same Little Cottonwood Canyon area where the exterior building materials for the Salt Lake Temple came from. (Some rumors maintained that the tower was built or at least commissioned by Brigham Young, but he died in 1877 and was not involved with it.)

The three-story tower was either 56 feet or 63 feet high (depending on what source you believe). It was about 25 feet in diameter and was said to be 312 feet higher than the intersection of Main Street and South Temple Street. Anderson patterned his tower after similar structures he had seen in Scotland. The tower had an observation area on the third story, as well as a telescope.

When the tower first opened, he charged admission to go to the top. The interest just wasn't great enough, and the tower soon closed and was somewhat neglected.

In May 1908, Anderson tried to revive interest in the tower. He offered free admission. The *Inter-Mountain Republican* newspaper stated on May 18, 1908, that some three thousand people visited the tower in a single day after

Anderson Tower as it appeared in the late nineteenth century on "C" Street on the north bench above downtown Salt Lake City. *Courtesy of Utah State Historical Society.*

its re-opening. The *Deseret Evening News* of May 16 stated that the tower was a landmark, now open again. It proclaimed it was "one of the show places of the city."

At least one newspaper ad for the tower contained totally sensationalized details. An advertisement in the *Deseret Evening News* of August 6, 1907, stated: "Anderson Tower was erected in early days for protection against the Indians." The tower remained open all day on Sundays and from 2:00 to

A plaque in a small park above Memory Grove commemorates Anderson Tower, a three-story granite structure that used to rise up in the area. *Author photo.*

5:00 p.m. on weekdays for some time, but again interest in it wore off. And vandalism was a continuing problem.

Tower Heights was a related nearby residential development in 1908, with homes costing more than $10,000 envisioned there.

Finally, the tower site was sold to Salt Lake City. The *Salt Lake Telegram* of October 15, 1930, stated that $7,200 purchased the property. The agreement was that it would be utilized as a city park and that nothing there would ever obstruct the view of City Creek Canyon and Memory Grove below. The tower was torn down about two years later, in 1932.

Today, that agreement is still honored. Only a small granite monument made from a piece of the tower remains. A steep stairway to the west leads down into Memory Grove, and technically, the tower property is an eastward extension of the park.

23

WHEN WELFARE EQUALED POOR FARMS

Almost a decade before Roy, Utah, received its name, Weber County had a poor farm in that locality on what was then known as the "Sandridge," or the "Ridge"

The *Salt Lake Herald* of July 21, 1887, reported: "Weber County has bought a poor farm. The farm consists of eighty acres near the Hooper switch on the Utah Central. The purchase is intended to furnish a self-supporting home for unfortunates who may be thrown upon the public charity."

The original farm encompassed eighty acres and was located just north of what today would be 2700 West and 5500 South (just west of the Union Pacific railroad tracks and east of the Rio Grande Rail Trail). It was purchased for $1,800. The farm was surrounded by a barbed-wire fence and included large fields of produce. There was a small house on the property, and more buildings were added later to accommodate the occupants, who were often referred to as "inmates." If a person in Weber County could not sustain themselves, they lived on the farm and worked as much as they were able to support themselves.

Roy, Utah, was settled in 1873, but it didn't even have a post office until 1894, so the poor farm predated that. Indeed, the first mention of Roy being the community with a poor farm was in the *Davis County Clipper* on August 26, 1910.

There was eventually a small cemetery on the property; if a resident died and had no other means of burial, they were interred there. There were likely twenty-five to thirty burials made over the decades there, though what eventually happened to the cemetery is unknown.

The Heritage Park, an assisted living center, sits on the site that was originally the "Poor Farm" in Roy for western Weber County. *Author photo.*

A June 6, 1911 report in the *Ogden Evening Standard* featured a visit by Weber County and Ogden area leaders to the poor farm in Roy. The leaders were challenged to eat the same lunch as the farm occupants, and they accepted the offer. The report from the poor farm cook was excellent, and no one went hungry. The poor farm was mentioned as having vegetable gardens and orchards, but no cattle, though some other poor farms in Utah did have herds.

By the early twentieth century, the poor farm became known as the Weber County Infirmary. A fire in 1921 destroyed the main building on the property. Later, Weber County sold off property and used it to create other facilities closer to Ogden City, then seven miles distant.

In 1960, the Weber County Chronic Disease Hospital opened. Then the name was changed to Weber Memorial Hospital. By the twenty-first century, the name was Heritage Park Rehabilitation and HealthCare Center. (One of my grandmothers, who lived in Hooper, often joked that she'd end up at the poor farm if she couldn't take care of herself. Sadly, when her heart began to fail at age ninety-three, she was placed in Weber Memorial Hospital—at the very site of the old poor farm—and she seemed to lament that before passing away a few months later.)

When the facility had transformed to the Weber Memorial Hospital status in the 1960s, it was the closest medical office to Hooper and all of western Roy.

Salt Lake County also had a poor farm. It was located somewhere south of Salt Lake City and was mentioned in a story in the *Salt Lake Herald* on August 25, 1889. Box Elder County also had its own poor farm, located on twenty acres, with many fruit trees, according to the *Brigham City Bugler* of August 1, 1890.

Cache County had a poor farm in Logan as well, according to the *Logan Journal* of June 8, 1892. Sanpete County in Manti also had a poor farm of forty acres, as reported by the *Salt Lake Tribune* on June 7, 1895.

According to the *Salt Lake Times* of August 31, 1892, Salt Lake County also used poor-farm residents to perform road work in order to save money on construction and street repairs.

There were poor farms all over the country during the same period.

The poor farms were all gone by World War II, replaced by sanitariums and other facilities. Then, today's welfare system came into prominence.

24

REDISCOVERING THE
"LAST LEAF ON THE TREE"

The Hooper, Utah Cemetery (Weber County) can rightfully brag about having the grave of the "Last Leaf on the Tree"—Mary Field Garner. She was the last living person who was acquainted with the Prophet Joseph Smith, first president of The Church of Jesus Christ of Latter-day Saints.

Is this not significant? After all, the key claim to fame of Clarkston, Utah, in Cache County, is that "The Man Who Knew"—Martin Harris, one of the Three Witnesses of the Book of Mormon—is buried in that City Cemetery. (This apparently obscure fact was uncovered in March 2021 by one of my sisters, Karen Arave Hugie. It was surprising news to her and me, as our parents, Gene and Norma Arave, were caretaker and sexton, respectively, of the Hooper, Utah Cemetery for some twenty-three years. And they never mentioned it or highlighted it. I'm sure some other Hooper residents may have known about it, but it was never recognized historically, as it should have been.)

A *Deseret News* story on August 21, 1943, by Bishop Marvin O. Ashton of the Church's Presiding Bishopric is the source of "The Last Leaf on the Tree" comparison. Mary Field Garner was born in England on February 1, 1836. She died at age 107 on July 20, 1943. At the time, she was believed to be the oldest ever member of the LDS Church. "At the time of the [Prophet's]) martyrdom she was eight years old and remembers vividly the day that people rose in their seats, when Brigham Young, as it were, was transfigured into the personality of the prophet," Bishop Ashton wrote in the *Deseret News*.

The headstone marker for Mary F. Garner, the final person alive to know Joseph Smith, first president of The Church of Jesus Christ of Latter-day Saints. *Author photo*.

This is the World War I cannon in the Hooper, Utah cemetery. The "Last Leaf on the Tree" grave is northwest of this monument. *Author photo*.

Ironically, she also had a rather embarrassing confession about that transfiguration story. She was tending an infant on her lap in that meeting. Her parents had brought a tin cup along as a plaything for the baby. Yet just as Brigham Young rose to his feet, the tin cup fell to the floor and created an embarrassing noise.

Sister Garner had lived in Slaterville but moved to Hooper and resided there for many years. It is there that her last five of ten children were born and where she passed away. (Some old newspaper stories incorrectly claim she lived in Roy, probably assuming that most people would not know where Hooper even was.)

To find the modest grave of Mary Field Garner, turn on the interior cemetery road heading east, just past and north of the two white buildings; When this road curves north, look for two tall upright markers just to the south of the curve, about thirty yards' distant. Her grave is a flat marker between them.

Of course, with 107 years of life, Sister Garner has a long, long story to tell of traveling across the plains to Utah and of the territory and the state's early history.

25

OGDEN VALLEY'S FORMER
ARTESIAN WELL PARK

W ater has always been a centerpiece of Ogden Valley. Before the days of Pineview Reservoir (before the mid-1930s), at the west end of the valley there were green meadows and many flowing artesian wells.

When the pioneers arrived in force in the 1860s, cattle roamed the area, and ranchers noticed cool waters bubbling up from the ground, likely near where the west end of Pineview Reservoir is today.

In 1889, the first artesian well was drilled, 84 feet down. It provided forty gallons a minute. Between then and 1935, a total of fifty-one wells were drilled, forty-eight of them flowing. The average depth of the wells was 135 feet, but the deepest went some 600 feet down.

Ogden City drilled the wells to augment its water supply. Ogden was already receiving water from the Weber and Ogden Rivers, plus from Taylor, Waterfall and Strongs Canyons. In 1925, there was a temporary sand problem in one of the new wells. But the 1920s heralded the artesian wells as a new summer tourist destination. The July 16, 1924 *Ogden Standard-Examiner* reported scores of inquiries a day to Ogden City from all over the nation about its artesian well park.

Indeed, that summer, the Ogden Chamber of Commerce regularly shuttled tourists to the wells. It also mailed out some ten thousand booklets that summer about the wells all over the country as a promotion. "Take a cool ride through Ogden Canyon stopping at Hermitage Inn and Park Pineview and Artesian Wells" read an advertisement in 1926 in the *Standard-Examiner*.

During the 1920s, the artesian well park in Ogden Valley was a popular tourist attraction. *Courtesy of Utah State Historical Society.*

Even before the first deep well was drilled, some types of simpler water fountains were there. The *Standard-Examiner* on March 25, 1888, reported, "It is worth the pains of the trip [up Ogden Canyon]) to get a drink from these fountains and enjoy the fresh, invigorating mountain air."

The city planted grass, trees and shrubs in 1922 at the well park and used cement to create standard circular fountains. You didn't visit Ogden Canyon or Ogden Valley without taking a cool drink from one of the flowing wells. The artesian wells soon provided 811,000 gallons a minute, or 16,000,000 gallons of water a day. The water was piped to Ogden in a redwood pipe, used for some fifty years.

The artesian wells soon formed Artesian Well Park, a refreshing summer spot for residents and tourists.

August 1933 saw the only dark side to the artesian wells, as some sort of contamination plagued the well water for part of that summer.

When Pineview Reservoir was filled in 1937, the artesian wells were capped and piped out to Ogden Canyon, to continue to supply drinking water to area residents. By 1956, two-thirds of Ogden's water, some twenty million gallons a day, were from the artesian wells.

However, it was realized in April 1968 that after three decades, the seventy-foot-deep reservoir water and accompanying pressures had damaged the piping and caused untreated Pineview water to seep into the drinking-water pipes. This turned the water red and created slime and odor problems with the water. All the Pineview water was then chlorinated for health reasons in that emergency. Unfortunately, the process killed most of the trout in the waters.

Pineview Dam was then drained, and the old artesian wells were capped. From December 1970 to May 1971, six new and larger artesian wells were dug above the high-water elevation of the reservoir—all about 260 feet deep—and funneled into a thirty-six-inch pipe that goes beneath Pineview Reservoir and into Ogden Canyon.

These supplied about as much water as the old forty-eight wells. According to Justin Anderson, Ogden City engineer, this newer artesian well field provides for 67 percent of the drinking water demand to Ogden City, as of 2015. During peak use, water from the Water Treatment Plant (just west of the base of Pineview Dam) is used to supplement the demand. "Along the Wasatch front it is not unusual for drinking water utilities to utilize well fields," Anderson stated. "The amount of water extracted from Ogden's well field is relatively large when compared to surrounding water systems."

Anderson also noted that the water rights associated with Ogden City's wells are some of the oldest in the surrounding area. So, although the original artesian well park has been gone for almost eight decades, refreshing waters from the same vast underground source in Ogden Valley still dominate Ogden's drinking water supply.

26

WHEN OGDEN BOASTED ITS OWN
TABERNACLE CHOIR

Ogden Tabernacle Choir to Sing in Salt Lake Tabernacle Tomorrow." That was an April 7, 1917 headline in the *Ogden Standard-Examiner*. Yes, Ogden boasted its own Tabernacle Choir for some eighty-six years in the past, and it often competed directly with the Salt Lake Tabernacle Choir.

The Ogden Choir had its own Ogden Tabernacle to sing in but also performed at times in General Conferences in the Salt Lake Tabernacle in the nineteenth century. "A Tabernacle Choir. It Was Thoroughly Organized Sunday Afternoon" was a March 10, 1891 *Ogden Standard* headline. Back then, Weber LDS Stake president Lewis Shurtliff stated that he desired "a thoroughly equipped and competent Tabernacle choir."

An even earlier *Standard* article, on June 20, 1881, reported that the Ogden Tabernacle Choir was enlarged, so it must have had even earlier beginnings. In fact, the book *Beneath Ben Lomond's Peak* states that the choir had its modest start as early as 1863, with just 12 voices. By 1896, it boasted 121 members.

The biggest rivalry came in early 1911, when it had to be decided which Mormon Tabernacle Choir, Ogden's or Salt Lake's, would represent the state during the ten-day National Land Show in New York's Madison Square Garden the following November and sing "Irrigation Ode." A lengthy *Standard* article on April 4, 1911, stated: "Presidency of Church Favors Ogden Choir." President Joseph F. Smith was reported to like the Ogden Choir for the show. The Ogden Choir had recently toured the

Ogden, Utah, temporarily had its own "Tabernacle Choir" in the early twentieth century. *Courtesy "Rededication History of the Ogden, Utah Temple 2014."*

western United States, singing at Portland or Sacramento, and they were "considered second to none."

Former Ogden mayor Fred J. Kiesel had lobbied the land show on behalf of the Ogden Choir. Willard Scowcroft, Joseph Ballantyne and Charles J. Ross had also worked hard promoting the choir. But the Salt Lake Mormon Tabernacle Choir landed the contract to sing in New York. "As Usual Zion Claims It All" was the April 5, 1911 *Standard* headline. The Ogden Tabernacle Choir toured San Diego and San Francisco in the 1920s and had many favorable reviews by the media in those cities.

Merlin Ray Sorensen wrote his 1961 thesis for the Brigham Young University Department of Music on Ogden's Tabernacle Choir history and concluded the choir was great publicity for not only the LDS Church but also for the State of Utah. (The Salt Lake Tabernacle Choir began its famed national radio broadcasts in 1929, further overshadowing Ogden's version of the choir.)

How many members were in the Ogden Choir about that time? Almost 150 members are shown in an April 7, 1917 choir photograph in the *Standard*. (Today's Mormon Tabernacle Choir has 360 members.)

How long did members sing in the Ogden Tab Choir? Some did so for decades. For example, Ivy Stanford Goddard Whitaker of Ogden sang in the choir from 1906 until it was disbanded in 1949. During World War II, the Ogden Choir dwindled to just one hundred members. In 1949, some former members joined the Ogden Oratorio Society.

It is also worth noting that Brigham City had its own Tabernacle Choir as well. A November 15, 1922 story in the *Standard* reported that "it is anticipated that the choir will become one of the leading choral organizations of the state."

Farmington and Provo also had Tabernacle Choirs, though Ogden's lasted longer than any except Salt Lake's. Since it could take the better part of a day to travel from Ogden to Salt Lake in the late nineteenth century, having separate Tabernacle Choirs was likely a geographical necessity.

But by the 1950s, there was only one world-renowned Mormon Tabernacle Choir: the Salt Lake Tabernacle Choir. Today, its choir members have to live within a one-hundred-mile radius of Salt Lake's Temple Square. Thus, Brigham City Church members—and even those in Logan—could meet that requirement.

27

THE MYSTERIOUS EDEN PARK

Eden Park, in Bountiful, is the most forgotten Utah resort of the nineteenth century. It was also the shortest-lived recreational spot of its era, lasting just a single season.

The first mention of Eden Park was in June 1894. The *Salt Lake Tribune* of June 12 reported that a naming contest was held and that "Eden Park" was chosen to be the new resort's title.

The park was constructed by Simon Bamberger, manager of the Great Salt Lake and Hot Springs Railroad (later simply called the Bamberger Railroad). Bamberger's Park and Bamdale were also suggested for the resort's name. Eden Park officially opened on June 16, 1894, and was designed to drive more traffic to Bamberger's railroad as it expanded northward.

The *Tribune* of June 13, 1894, stated that music, dancing, a bowery, refreshments and nighttime illumination were key features of the three-acre Eden Park.

The *Davis County Clipper* of June 14, 1894, described Eden Park as a pleasure resort near Stoker Station, featuring picnicking, fruit and shade trees, plus a new drinking water artesian well. From Salt Lake City, it was thirty-five cents for a round-trip train ride and admission to the park for adults. (It was twenty cents for children). There were six round-trip passenger trains a day, requiring about thirty minutes each way.

On June 21, 1894, the *Clipper* reported: "The indications are that before the summer has past that Eden Park will be among the foremost of Utah's pleasure resorts. Last Saturday the evening train for Salt Lake was made of

The Bamberger rail line, here shown in 1937, was built in the 1890s and first accessed the short-lived Eden Park resort in Bountiful. *Courtesy of Utah State Historical Society.*

six coaches all of which were crowded….A band from Salt Lake plays in the pavilion each afternoon. A force of men are still at work completing and beautifying the park." (Few if any photographs of Eden Park exist.)

The *Salt Lake Tribune* of June 24, 1894, reported that a grand masquerade ball was to be held there on June 26. Some four hundred patrons a day were reported visiting the resort each day. The park also had swings and a baseball field. Professor Peterson's Orchestra often played there. The *Tribune* of July 3 stated that barbecued oxen was to be a holiday food highlight there.

The *Salt Lake Herald* of August 7, 1894, noted that an Eden Park road race was scheduled to go from Salt Lake City to the park and that an observatory train would shadow the footrace.

The *Davis County Clipper* on September 12, 1952, looked back at the resort and stated that it was located at the bottom of Barton Creek, on the east side of the railroad tracks.

The *Clipper* of March 28, 1895, reported that the Eden Park pavilion had been moved that month to a hot springs. (The nearest two hot springs were on Beck Street in Salt Lake.) So the Bountiful garden resort lasted just a single season, in 1894.

As Simon Bamberger moved the Lake Park resort in west Farmington northeastward to its current site by Lagoon in 1895, that spelled doom for Eden Park. At an approximate halfway point between Salt Lake and Ogden, Lagoon resort was an ideal location and was Bamberger's focus thereafter. Lagoon opened in July 1886.

A shrinking Great Salt Lake meant the briny water was a full mile from Lake Park resort's facilities by 1895, making it unappealing to lake bathers who wanted to "float like a cork" in the salt-laden waters. (Only Saltair resort survived into the twentieth century along the Great Salt Lake.)

Notwithstanding the receding waters, Lake Park had always had a mud problem along its shore. The *Salt Lake Herald* of July 31, 1910, reported that no amount of gravel, sand or fill could overcome that vexing problem.

In that era of the late nineteenth and early twentieth centuries, "resorts" were not the thrill-ride-dominated parks they are today. They were basically shady picnicking areas with tables, dancing, music and sporting activities. Lagoon didn't receive its first ride (beyond the "Shoot the Chutes" activity of sliding wooden sleds down an incline and into lake water) until 1906, when the carousel arrived. The wooden roller coaster didn't come along until 1921, the same year as the opening of a cement swimming pool.

28

FORERUNNER TO FRONTRUNNER

Bamberger Rail Line

efore today's FrontRunner, there was the Bamberger Railroad Line. FrontRunner, today's light rail line in northern Utah, opened on April 26, 2008, after three years of construction. (It added more stops in 2012 and thereafter.) The Bamberger basically followed today's I-15 corridor and ran for more than sixty years until 1952, when the popularity of the automobile put it out of business.

After a fifty-six-year gap, FrontRunner came along. Here is the story of the Bamberger Railroad, forerunner of FrontRunner.

The Bamberger Railroad, a thirty-six-mile railroad line, connected Salt Lake City and Ogden with more than thirty major stops until the last car ran in September 1952. While the Bamberger wasn't the only trolley transportation system in Utah, it was the first and most successful. (A sixty-six-mile Salt Lake–Payson trolley system operated from 1916 to 1946. There was a "Saltair" line, too.)

Simon Bamberger, a successful Utah businessman and later governor, received the first shipment of light rail near the Union Pacific Railroad Station in Salt Lake City in 1891. Existing railroads were concerned with through traffic, not with serving small communities, as Bamberger was.

The line's original name was the Great Salt Lake and Hot Springs Railway. Not until 1917 was the name changed to the Bamberger Electric Railroad. The line converted from steam power to electricity in 1910, ushering in the "trolley" era.

The Bamberger railroad line in Ogden, Utah, probably in the late 1940s. The line operated from 1891 to 1952. *Courtesy of Utah State Historical Society.*

Line construction reached Farmington in 1895, and that's when Bamberger purchased the old buildings at Lake Shore Resort and moved them east to a swampy area that he turned into a recreational paradise, Lagoon. Free admission to Lagoon was given to all railroad users. Lagoon stimulated railroad use, especially in the summer.

Davis was the only high school in Davis County while the Bamberger operated, and students used to ride the railroad before school buses were purchased. An extra dozen rail cars were needed to take students to the high school, and these cars were stored in Kaysville until needed again at the end of the school day. The school district paid the railroad for the students' transportation.

Other steady passengers on the railway were employees of the Davis County School District, the Farmington Courthouse, the Kaysville Brick Company and Miller Floral. "Hop the Bamberger" was the familiar phrase used in conjunction with the orange-and-cream-colored cars. The rail line reached Kaysville in 1903, Layton in 1904, Sunset in 1905 and Ogden in 1908.

The Depression hurt the railroad's business, but it survived. It also lived through the flood of 1923, which wiped out the line through Farmington and Centerville. World War II was a boon to the Bamberger. The line had exclusive service to Hill Field (Hill Air Force Base), increasing its passenger service threefold and its freight load by eight times. Passenger service in 1945 was the company's highest, with revenues jumping from $413,000 in 1939 to $2,000,000 in 1945.

Normal Bamberger passenger service had been from 6:00 a.m. to midnight, but the war necessitated service around the clock. Tickets could be purchased by several methods, destination to destination or by the mile.

According to research by the Kaysville-Layton Historical Society, some passengers used to joke, "The Bamberger went 100 mph—90 up and down and 10 forward."

Some of the old track rails for the Bamberger still existed along portions of Ogden's Wall Avenue well into the 1970s.

The main stops along the Bamberger were as follows: Ogden, Lincoln Avenue, just north of Twenty-Fourth Street; Cozydale, 4400 South 1500 West; Roy, near 4800 South; Sunset, 1800 North, just east of I-15; Arsenal, 1300 North, just east of I-15; Clearfield, 700 South, east of I-15; Robbins, 2200 North, I-15, Layton; Allen, 1000 North, I-15, Layton; Davis High School, Kaysville; Lagoon, Farmington; Glover's Lane, Farmington; Chase Lane, Centerville; Centerville, 400 South 150 West; Thomas, 100 North Center, Bountiful; Bountiful, 200 West 200 South; Parkin, 800 North U-89, North Salt Lake; Cleverly, 700 North U-89, North Salt Lake; Odell, 450 North U-89, North Salt Lake; Everett, 1455 North 700 West, Salt Lake County; and Salt Lake Depot, West Temple and South Temple, on present-day Abravanel Hall site.

29

"GIANT RACER"

Saltair's Legendary Roller Coaster

When most Utahns think of roller coasters, they think of Lagoon. That's where the state's only coasters are now. But it's not where Utah's first roller coaster was. The king of Utah roller coasters was the late "Giant Racer" of Saltair, which reigned supreme for sixty-four years. Unfortunately, you'd have to have been born before 1950 to have ridden the Racer, as a freak wind gust destroyed it in 1957.

Details on the Giant Racer are sketchy, but during the 1920s it was reputed to be "the world's longest wooden roller coaster." Its height is definitely known to have been 110 feet. To put that into perspective, Lagoon's current wooden roller coaster (opened in 1921) is only 45 feet high. (One of its steel coasters, Cannibal, is 208 feet high.)

There were apparently three versions of the Giant Racer. The first might have opened as early as 1893, when Saltair itself premiered. Then, by either 1916 or 1919, the coaster was improved significantly.

A large fire at Saltair in 1931 destroyed the Giant Racer. It was rebuilt within a year for $70,000. This third version had two peaks, both 110 feet high, as well as eight other hills to climb.

Historical accounts say the Racer went so fast after that first drop that brakes were always applied going up the second hill to slow it down. How fast was it? There's no official account, but it probably rolled at about fifty-five miles per hour. (Compare that to forty-five miles per hour for Lagoon's wooden coaster and seventy miles per hour for its Cannibal coaster.)

Top: The "Giant Racer" wooden roller coaster at Saltair was a key attraction at the Great Salt Lake resort. *Courtesy of Utah State Historical Society.*

Bottom: The "Giant Racer" as it appeared in the 1950s at Saltair. The coaster opened in 1932 and closed in August 1957. *Courtesy of Utah State Historical Society.*

Wooden roller coasters, although not as fast as modern steel ones, have an added thrill. The wood gives just enough to create a shaking sort of thrill. "That was one wild ride," said former Kaysville City councilman Stephen Whitesides in recalling one of his rides on the Giant Racer.

Former *Deseret News* business writer Roger Pusey agreed, saying it took the company of a beautiful girl as a date to persuade him to ride it. "It was enough to make my heart come up to my tonsils," said Joe Liddell of Tooele. "It was a great thing to take your date on." He also said it was a nice way to get away from the mosquitoes, which were an annoyance around the rest of Saltair.

One old advertisement for the Giant Racer called it "the ride through the clouds." Another said it was "one of the dizziest in the world."

Because the coaster had parallel tracks, coaster trains would often race each other through the almost mile-long ride.

The Giant Racer met an untimely demise on August 30, 1957, when an estimated seventy-five-mile-per-hour wind gust toppled 60 percent of the coaster's framework, including its two high points. The framework is described as toppling like broken matchsticks. But no one was hurt. Fortunately, because of heavy rain, the Giant Racer had been closed at 3:00 p.m. that fateful day, two hours before the wind gust struck.

The wind damage was $100,000, and Saltair could not afford to rebuild it. Saltair itself closed in 1959, and the entire complex burned to the ground in 1970, destroying anything that may have remained of the Giant Racer. However, most of the remains of the coaster had been dismantled in the early 1960s.

Unfortunately, the third and current version of Saltair didn't include a roller coaster.

IV

What-Ifs That Could Have Been

THE MISSING TEN FLOORS
IN THE SALT LAKE SKYLINE

The twenty-eight-story Church Office Building for the Church of Jesus Christ of Latter-day Saints soars above North Temple Street, where it has been the nerve center for the Church since the late 1960s. However, the 420-foot-tall building was originally planned to be much taller.

Although the Joseph Smith Memorial Building directly honors the first president of the Church, the Church Office Building was originally envisioned to do so first, with a planned thirty-eight floors, to commemorate the thirty-eight years of Joseph Smith's life.

The thirty-eight floors didn't materialize, for a variety of reasons. If the plan had been realized, the building would have soared to more than five hundred feet. So, what happened to the additional ten stories?

J. Howard Dunn, who was in charge of project development for the Church's building committee, said in a 1962 *Church News* article that the plans were changed and eight stories were scrapped to better meet mechanical requirements of the engineering department. Heating and air-conditioning for the skyscraper would best be handled in fourteen-story units, beginning above the first two floors. At that time, the high-rise was to be thirty stories. Later, two more stories were eventually deleted from that plan.

The building height was reduced for two other reasons as well. First, construction began on the Granite Records Vault in Little Cottonwood Canyon in 1960 and reduced the need for downtown office building space. Second, departing missionaries were to be housed elsewhere, again reducing required space.

This is the twenty-eight-story office building of the Church of Jesus Christ of Latter-day Saints. The building was originally proposed to be ten stories taller. *Author photo*.

The original plans called for housing space for up to 430 outgoing missionaries in the first few floors of the Church Office Building. As it turned out, missionaries were housed across the street to the north in an old school until the Missionary Training Center opened in Provo in 1978. (Missionaries were still fed in the Church Office Building cafeteria in the early 1970s.)

The Church Office Building cost $31.4 million (the equivalent of more than $200 million today). The new building led to the substantial widening of North Temple and State Streets. "The building is designed for immediate and future needs of the church," Mark B. Garff, chairman of the building committee, told the *Deseret News* in 1969.

George Cannon Young designed the building, which was under design as early as 1961. The old Deseret Gymnasium, at 37 East South Temple, had to be relocated across the street to where the Conference Center is now. Some Church Business College buildings and other structures also had to be moved to make room.

Work on the three-story, underground, 1,400-space parking structure— Utah's largest building excavation at the time—began in 1962 and was finished by about 1967. The extracted dirt, 250,000 cubic yards, provided fill material for original I-15 construction in Salt Lake County.

When completed, the building also allowed the Church to temporarily house all General Authorities there while doing a substantial remodel of the Church Administration Building at 47 East South Temple.

THE MYSTERY OF OGDEN'S
CENTURY TEMPLE WAIT

Why did Ogden, the State of Utah's second-largest city for well over a century, have to wait more than one hundred years for a temple?

Well, it was simply because it was Ogden. Yes, Ogden was that "railroad town" that first brought the liberals, the unions, non-Mormon mayors and others into northern Utah. It was first settled in the late 1840s.

Ogden-area church members actually helped construct and finance the Salt Lake Temple, which was completed in 1893. (The town of Logan, to the north, wasn't settled until 1859 yet had its own temple by 1884.)

By the early twentieth century, Ogden-area church members were eager for their own temple. Indeed, a headline in the *Ogden Standard-Examiner* on December 13, 1920, read, "Ogden to Get Temple, Mormons Are Told."

Church members at the North Weber Stake quarterly conference were informed by Church patriarch Hyrum G. Smith that Ogden would have a temple in the "near future." Patriarch Smith mentioned the overcrowding in the Salt Lake Temple and challenged members to be ready for new construction of both a tabernacle and a temple.

However, in 1921, Church president Heber J. Grant made a special visit to Ogden and left indicating that it was not the proper time to have a temple there. An article in the *Deseret News* on May 16, 1921, reported, "A temple site was inspected in this city early Sunday morning by Presidents Heber J. Grant and Anthony W. Ivins, together with local Church officials."

Lester Park, 663 Twenty-Fourth Street in Ogden, was once offered by Ogden City leaders to the LDS Church as a possible Ogden Temple site. *Liz Arave Hafen photo*.

The Joseph Clark family had approached the LDS Church about donating land near Thirtieth Street and Tyler, on just one condition: that an Ogden Temple be erected on the property one day. The land at Thirtieth and Tyler already had a religious history. In the year 1890, a Methodist university, dubbed "Utah University," was being built at the same address.

The entire first floor of the university's main building was constructed by 1891, before financial problems and some national shakeups within the Methodist Church doomed that project. The land was eventually returned to its original owners, the Clark family. Thirty years later, they sought to donate it for a temple site.

Ogden resident Carla Vogel, who grew up at Thirty-Second Street and Iowa in Ogden in the 1930s and 1940s, said her father knew the Clark family well and always maintained that the actual site the Clarks had in mind for an Ogden Temple was on the hill and to the east above Thirtieth and Tyler, where St. Benedict's Hospital was opened in 1946. She said that lofty site meant a large portion of the city would be able to see the temple. (Likely the reason the Thirtieth and Tyler address was given in the articles was because, in the 1920s, there was no real development above and to the east of that location.)

This is the original version of the Ogden Temple, under construction in the late 1960s. *Courtesy "Rededication History of the Ogden, Utah Temple 2014."*

The 1921 *Deseret News* article also stated: "A movement has been on foot for a temple for this city for some time past, owing to the great amount of activity of Church members in genealogical and temple work and the fact that only limited numbers can now be accommodated at the Salt Lake Temple. President Grant...announced that from $2 million to $3 million were now on application for other purposes and there was no telling when a temple could be built in Ogden."

President Grant also lectured Ogden-area church members, proclaiming that if every member paid a full tithing, many more temples could be readily built, like one in Ogden. Furthermore, Grant identified Ogden's Lester Park (663 Twenty-Fourth Street, where today's Weber County Main Library sits) as better suited for a temple site.

One of those Church-planned projects, a $300,000 Deseret Gymnasium in Ogden, was already on the drawing board, and it was completed in 1925. Area wards were assessed amounts to pay for the gym, and it was implied that after that debt was paid, a temple would be next to come. Indeed, a February 10, 1924 headline in the *Standard-Examiner* was, "L.D.S. Members Looking Forward to New Temple and Larger Tabernacle."

"That a temple may be built in Ogden within a few years is the fond hope of the large number of temple workers who are making regular visits to the Salt Lake and Logan temples," the story stated. "A temple in Ogden would mean more temple work performed by local church people at less expense, as transportation expenses would then be eliminated."

On May 7, 1924, the *Standard* reported that the Associated Clubs of Ogden had written to President Grant about trading Tabernacle Square Park (site of today's LDS Temple/Tabernacle) for Lester Park. The purpose of the trade was to provide "a suitable site for an Ogden temple."

That proposal was also turned down by the LDS Church. Again, this illustrates how some LDS Church leaders did not favor the area, likely letting the presence of liberal non-Mormons in Ogden supersede the fact there were many faithful LDS members residing there as well. (In the early 1890s, the LDS Church had actually given Ogden City the deed to the property that is now Tabernacle Square. But the city decided it could not properly care for the property, and it was given back to the Church a few years later. The *Standard* declared on December 20, 1893: "The City Gives It Up. City Council Gives Back the Tabernacle Square to the Church.")

This aerial view shows the original Ogden Temple and Tabernacle, probably in the early twenty-first century. *Courtesy "Rededication History of the Ogden, Utah Temple 2014."*

The original Ogden Temple opened on January 18, 1972, in downtown Ogden City. *Courtesy "Rededication History of the Ogden, Utah Temple 2014."*

In 1929, the Great Depression hit, and in late 1941, World War II came along—two other factors likely not in Ogden's favor for gaining a temple. On February 12, 1956, Ogden did receive a new tabernacle, the last such new tabernacle to be built in the Church (not counting the future Conference Center in Salt Lake).

But even having Church president David O. McKay in the 1950s hailing from nearby Huntsville, in Ogden Valley, didn't seem to help Ogden's temple void very much.

Through the middle part of the twentieth century, Ogden-area Church members were actually a part of the Logan Temple District, and many wards/stakes chartered evening bus trips to that temple in the 1960s. That was a difficult trip in winter, with mountainous Sardine Canyon to traverse into Cache County.

Above: The rebuilt Ogden Temple is shown under construction in August 2012. *Courtesy "Rededication History of the Ogden, Utah Temple 2014."*

Left: The completed second version of the Ogden Temple as pictured in 2014. *Author photo.*

By the mid-1960s, Ogden was still Utah's second-largest city, with a population of almost sixty-nine thousand. Almost half were LDS Church members, but still no temple was built in Ogden until 1972. And Ogden received a new temple (when Provo also did) primarily because two new temples would cost less than expanding the Logan and Manti Temples.

32

WHEN LONE PEAK
COULD HAVE BEEN DYNAMITED

C ould Lone Peak have been destroyed or marred by a dynamite blast in 1937? "Will Dynamite Crash Hilltop(?)" was the headline of an Associated Press story in the *Ogden Standard-Examiner* of August 19, 1937. The story stated, "Lone Peak, lofty outcropping of the Wasatch range upon which a great airliner crashed last winter, is to be blasted at its tip into a tomb for the tragedy that claimed seven lives."

On December 15, 1936, a Western Air Express Boeing 247 crashed just below Hardy Ridge on Lone Peak. Most of the aircraft was hurled over the ridge and dropped over one thousand feet into the basin below.

Lone Peak, a summit at 11,253 feet above sea level in the Wasatch Mountains, is located east of Draper. (Strictly speaking, Hardy Ridge is located hundreds of yards south of Lone Peak, above Hardy Lake.)

The Associated Press story stated that Western Air Express had secured permission from the U.S. Forest Service to dynamite the mountaintop. This was in order to "bury the crash area which now attracts sight-seers and which, because of frequent rock slides, is considered a menace." The story reported that the seven bodies, luggage, mail and plane parts were recovered after six months of searching followed by two months of digging and removal work.

It does not appear that Lone Peak itself was ever dynamited. No reports of such a blast could be found in old newspapers or via Google searches. But at least one person who read this report said a book on the history of the plane crash does mention that dynamite was indeed used to cover up the

The top tier of Lone Peak, a mountain 11,253 feet above sea level, just east of Draper, Utah. *Author photo.*

crash site. (The Lone Peak area includes a lot of unstable-looking rock, so an explosion could have altered the appearance of the area.)

In any event, according to the website Lost Flights (www.lostflights.com), Amelia Earhart herself participated in the search for the plane early on, but it wasn't located until July 1937 (the month Earhart disappeared).

There have been four deaths on Lone Peak in recent years, two from lightning strikes and two from falls off cliffs.

Notwithstanding the Lone Peak area's disastrous plane crash, it has always been a popular hiking destination. "Teachers Climb Peak" was a September 6, 1915 headline in the *Salt Lake Telegram*. The story said that fifteen principals and teachers from the Jordan School District climbed the peak on Labor Day weekend. They faced a heavy wind and snowstorm halfway up the mountain.

The *American Fork Citizen* of September 8, 1923, stated that six men climbed Lone Peak, also on Labor Day weekend. They camped overnight and had a large fire that could be seen from all over the area. "Wasatch Mountain Club Hikers Ascend Lone Peak" was an August 4, 1925 headline in the *Salt Lake Telegram*. A party of fourteen took three days to complete the hike. The *Telegram* of October 3, 1938, declared, "Hikers Climb Peak to Set New Record." Wasatch Mountain Club members Odell Pedersen, W.C. Kamp, Orson Spencer and Keith Anderson climbed the peak in three hours and fifty-eight minutes, one of the speediest times ever. And three members of the club scaled Lone Peak from the east side, which includes a seven-hundred-foot wall of granite. They did it in July 1958, according to the *Midvale Sentinel*.

SOUTH FORK

Utah's Abandoned Reservoir Site

I magine the South Fork of the Ogden River without all or most of its campgrounds and picnic areas. No Bott, South Fork, Perception Park, Meadows, Willow or perhaps even Magpie picnic and camping areas. No tubing or fishing most of the South Fork River. It almost happened.

That's because in November 1912, full-scale work began "on Big South Fork Dam," according to the *Standard-Examiner* of November 16 that year. (Some preliminary work had been done in 1911.) After forty years of dreaming about a dam on the South Fork, machinery was working there.

Bishop W.S. Steward of Plain City had previously spent considerable money in the South Fork area, trying to find a suitable dam location, but had given up. Others had tried as well. Only a revival of support by former Ogden mayor and *Standard-Examiner* publisher William Glasmann had pushed the idea forward again.

Fifty men armed with powder, steam and machinery began to prepare the site for concrete work. This dam was envisioned as being able to double Ogden and the area's population and serve water needs for one hundred years.

Where exactly was this dam started? At the confluence of Cobble Creek along the South Fork, or near today's South Fork Campground.

The proposed earthen dam was estimated to cost $1 million ($24 million in 2023 value) and initially rise 120 feet, eventually 200 feet. It would have had a storage capacity of 50,000 acre-feet. (Pineview is 110,000 acre-feet.) "The camp at the dam presents a busy scene and the place is a tented city," the *Standard* reported.

A postcard from 1924 shows the Wheeler Dam in Ogden Canyon, located adjacent to Wheeler Canyon. *Courtesy D. Boyd Crawford collection.*

The dam was eventually a joint project between Ogden City and the Ogden River Reservoir Company. Electric power generation was also planned. But the project was controversial, and a March 23, 1911 *Standard* article called a meeting on the South Fork dam the most important ever held in Weber County. (In this era, there was no Pineview or Causey Reservoir, only a small dam at the head of Wheeler Canyon in Ogden Canyon.)

"The people in Huntsville looked with surprise at the big gasoline engine hauling seven tons at a time through that town," the *Standard* reported.

What happened to the dam? It was eventually determined that the core wall was located on a fault plain. Also, while the south end wall hit bedrock, the other side did not. Blasting revealed an almost bottomless mud plain. Plans were even revised to take the dam about one and two-tenths miles downstream to the west, but additional shortcomings on a suitable foundation and delays, changes and politics in construction doomed the project.

"Reservoir Site Abandoned," was a November 22, 1912 headline in the *Standard*. That proved to be somewhat premature, as some work on the possible dam was still being done in 1913 and in the late winter of 1914. The project was on and off again many times.

As a sidelight, some of the first moving pictures ever seen by Ogden-area residents came in the fall of 1913. "Moving Pictures of Fashion Show and Big Dam" declared the October 22, 1913 *Standard*. Images of work on

A group of young adults tube down the South Fork of the Ogden River in the summer of 2018. *Author photo.*

the South Fork Dam were shown at the Globe Theater, 2530 Washington Avenue. "The picture of the big dynamite explosion at the dam site is interesting," the article stated.

As recent as May 18, 1923, the *Standard* reported government officials still mulling the South Fork of the Ogden River as a possible dam site. Interestingly, then, one site was called "Magpie Reservoir," with potential for a two-hundred-foot-high dam (likely the location of today's Magpie Campground).

By 1926, Echo Reservoir in Weber Canyon was started, and then the Great Depression struck in 1929. By the 1930s, the Federal Bureau of Reclamation controlled all dam construction, and it started Pineview Reservoir in 1934 in Ogden Valley itself.

In 1966, Causey Reservoir was completed. It is on the South Fork of the Ogden River. It also included some of Skull Crack Canyon, another potential dam site explored in the 1920s.

Still, you've got to wonder: If the South Fork Dam had been built in the 1910s, where would today's South Fork campgrounds be? What about Highway 39's route? Would Pineview and Causey Reservoirs still have been built the same, or at all?

A WEST DAVIS HIGHWAY IN 1948?

Many people might erroneously believe that a West Davis Highway corridor was first proposed by Utah governor Mike Leavitt in 1996, almost exactly twenty-one years before the Utah Department of Transportation announced its corridor for such a major highway.

However, "Davis Urges Wider Road, Inter-Regional Highway" was a December 3, 1948 headline in the *Davis County Clipper*. Thus, some forty-eight years earlier than when Governor Leavitt announced this regional highway, it had been first proposed.

That *Clipper* story stated that such a road should cross Farmington Bay before "skirting Davis County towns to the west." In northern Davis County, the story said, the road would follow the old Mormon Pioneer trail corridor, aka the Bluff Road (essentially where UDOT's modern four-lane highway is). "Purpose of this highway will be to rid the incorporated towns of Davis County of nuisance traffic, such as through traffic," the 1948 story said.

At the time, it was stated that the road would tie into Salt Lake City's Seventh West Street. On the north end, it would connect with Ogden's Twenty-Fourth Street Viaduct.

It was noted that the road would add three to four miles to the overall distance between Salt Lake and Ogden with the looping westward. Yet it was believed that this could be a bargain in future years, when development slows the speed limits on Highway 91, then the main corridor through Davis County. (I-15 didn't come along until the mid-1960s.)

Opposite, top: The original cement highway between Layton and Clearfield as it appeared in the late 1920s. *Courtesy of Heritage Museum of Layton.*

Opposite, bottom: The original paved main highway as it passed by the business district of Layton City in the 1920s. *Courtesy of Heritage Museum of Layton.*

Above: The West Davis Highway, near Gentile Street in Syracuse, under construction in 2021. Such a highway was first proposed in 1948. *LeAnn Arave photo.*

Purchasing the necessary right-of-way as soon as possible was stressed as the key to making the highway affordable. Of course, the road never happened and was off the radar for nearly another half century.

The *Clipper* story also mentioned that a "scenic highway" should be built from Farmington to Bountiful along the mountainside. UDOT did another study on a possible "West Davis Highway" in the early 1960s, but no other action was taken.

On July 16, 1996, Governor Leavitt announced his "Legacy Project"— the Western Transportation Corridor—at a press conference in West Haven. The *Deseret News* of July 17, 1996, reported:

> *This proposed highway would eventually stretch more than 130 miles, from North Ogden to Nephi, spanning five counties. "We have not determined the exact route for most of this," Gov. Leavitt said, though he specifically said it would run in the vicinity of 5600 South in Salt Lake County. It would definitely parallel I-15 from Farmington to Centerville and could run either side of Lake Mountain in Utah County. The map the Utah Department of Transportation presented at the conferences had no specific roadway identified—only a wide corridor.*

It was July 6, 2017, when UDOT announced the specific route for its nineteen-mile section of West Davis Highway after many years of debate with the cities and counties it passes through. The *Deseret News* of July 6 reported: "The route from Farmington to West Point would connect with I-15 and Legacy Parkway at Glovers Lane on the south end, and at state Route 37, or 1800 North, at approximately 4000 West on the north end." From Syracuse northward, it would follow the Bluff Road corridor, a section that West Point and Clinton have preserved very well from development over the last two decades.

The new West Davis Highway is planned to open in the summer of 2024.

35

WHEN CEDAR BREAKS HAD
A TRAIL DOWNWARD

C edar Breaks and Bryce Canyon were in a hot competition in the early twentieth century. When it was over, Bryce won and gained National Park status, while Cedar Breaks remains a National Monument to this day.

The two parks are somewhat similar. But Bryce Canyon has many trails downward that penetrate its interior, while Cedar Breaks has none.

It didn't used to be that way. According to the *Beaver County News* of July 15, 1927, there used to be a trail downward in Cedar Breaks. The reported stated:

> *At present comparatively few viewers of the Breaks follow a guide down the uncertain trails of the scalloped slopes into the midst of the columns, corridors, painted buttresses, colonnades, natural bridges, stairways, organs, alabaster shrines, altars, sculptured figures of fauns, satyrs, eagles, lions, Christian martyrs, Gothic cathedrals, and Grecian temples. Only a trip to the bottom can impress one with the full immensity, variety, and grandeur of the Cedar Breaks. But to me the most inspiring views are seen from Point Perfection and Point Supreme of the rim from which the out-flung bastions, buttresses, towers, parapets and craggy spires are not lost in the symphony of color the delightful pink and white of the terraces mingled with tints of orange, yellow, lavender, purple, ivory, ruby and vermilion in all their intermediate shadings. One is reminded of ancient Greece and Rome by the glorified temples and acropolises moldering in rosy marbled ruins, the report concluded.*

Cedar Breaks National Monument is shown in 1920. *Courtesy of Utah State Historical Society.*

So, it is likely that this only trail, perhaps even precarious in its prime, is gone, probably eroded away, because it was not maintained.

There is a long path into Cedar Breaks from below, from the Cedar City side. This path begins at the Crystal Springs Trailhead, about seven miles east of Cedar City, along Highway 14. It is fourteen to eighteen miles round-trip and strenuous.

36

WHEN UTAH ALMOST HAD
AN ALCATRAZ ISLAND

I n 1922, there was a proposal to move the prison the first time, from its original location (where Sugar House Park is now) to Antelope Island. "State Prison May Be Moved" was a September 28, 1922 headline in the *Ogden Standard-Examiner*.

Utah governor Charles R. Mabey appointed a commission to study that possibility. Of course, it never happened, but even in the 1920s, a prison encircled by residential neighborhoods was not deemed desirable. Antelope Island, undeveloped, could have made a kind of "Alcatraz Island" in the Top of Utah.

At about the same time, the mid-1920s, Edward Fenton Colburn of Salt Lake City had dreams of turning Antelope Island into a full-scale resort. He had plans to build a concrete bridge to the island, install bathing facilities there, as well as cottages, sports grounds and even a game preserve. Colburn, a Salt Lake judge, was trying to secure financing for such a resort when he died on January 14, 1926. His dreams apparently died with him.

But Colburn wasn't the first to envision Antelope Island as a resort. J.E. Dooly, president of the Antelope Island Improvement Company, spoke of possible recreational facilities there in 1910. He wanted a four-mile-long railroad spur to access the isle and even a loop of iron rails to encircle Antelope.

Some Utah Methodists even earlier, in 1888, had dreams of a "Utah Chautauqua" (an adult education movement featuring entertainment and culture) on Antelope Island, also with access to the railroad. But it was

Taylor Arave poses atop a large rock on Fremont Island in the Great Salt Lake. Antelope Island is shown in the distance. *Author photo*.

determined that there wasn't a high enough population base in the area to support that idea.

Antelope Island was originally called Church Island, starting in 1849, when the Church of Jesus Christ of Latter-day Saints started ranching operations there. The isle was referred to as Buffalo Island in the early twentieth century, when bison were placed there.

37

THE ORIGINAL LACKLUSTER TITLE
FOR ANGELS LANDING

P lace-naming was hit-and-miss in the early days of national parks. Sometimes, the most popular names replaced original titles of park features. Apparently, that is what happened with Zion National Park's Angels Landing.

According to a detailed account in the *Gunnison Valley News* of February 8, 1934, this park monolith was originally named "El Gobernador." This name was in honor of Utah's governor at the time, William Spry. He was Utah's third governor and served from 1909 to 1917. The article cites both P.P. Patraw, Zion National Park superintendent in the 1930s, and J. Cecil Alter, secretary of the Utah Historical Society, as finding documentation to verify the claim.

Dr. J.K.W. Braken of Salt Lake City, along with Douglas White, then editor of *Arrowhead* magazine, gave the park summit the name "El Gobernador" in 1913. Both men were members of a party organized by Governor Spry to visit Zion. Lawrence S. Marigan, president of the Salt Lake Transportation Company, also verified the peak's original name, since he was also a member of the visiting party in 1913. "Mr. Marigan states that Governor Spry knew of the error, but modestly refrained from saying anything about it," the article stated. It further stated that some historical accounts mistakenly credited El Gobernador as being an alternate name for the Great White Throne, located just across the canyon.

The 1913 touring group spent most of a day in Zion, touring it over sandy and rough roads. The group traveled into Zion as far north as the

Angels Landing is shown as it appears from the northwest side, from Scout Lookout. The formation originally had a different title. *Roger Arave photo*.

Temple Sinawava, where today's Gateway to the Narrows trail begins. It was afternoon when the party retraced their route, and it was late afternoon when they stopped past near today's Grotto Picnic area and noticed that the sun was illuminating the unnamed summit, which they called "El Gobernador," though some of the party thought it reminded them of Yosemite's El Capitan.

Douglas White even delivered a dedication speech on the newly named pinnacle. Later, a park sign was prepared with "El Gobernador," but somehow, by accident, the sign ended up below the Great White Throne and not the correct feature.

Four years later, *Arrowhead* magazine made a similar mistake when it named the Great White Throne "El Gobernador" in a mistitled caption. (Sadly, the "El" name didn't stick for the Great White Throne either.)

Where did the Angels Landing name come from?

Frederick Vining Fisher, an Ogden resident and former pastor of the First Methodist Episcopal Church of Ogden, named many rock monuments during a visit there in 1916 (or perhaps even earlier, in 1914, as one early Zion Park brochure from the late 1930s claims.)

Fisher, actually an early non-Mormon apologist, made a trip up Zion Canyon (then called either "Little Zion," "The Heavenly City of God" or "Mukuntuweap" ("straight canyon" to the Southern Paiute Indians). Fisher was accompanied by two locals, Rockville LDS bishop David Hirschi and his son Claude Hirschi.

The afternoon sun gloriously illuminated the Great White Throne and inspired Fisher to reportedly say: "Never have I seen such a sight before. It is by all odds America's masterpiece. Boys, I have looked for this mountain all my life but I never expected to find it in this world. This mountain is the Great White Throne."

Dr. Fisher (then going by an educational, rather than a religious title) also noticed a large rock formation on the opposite side of the narrow canyon, just northwest of the Great White Throne, and once again made a religious connection. He surmised that angels would never land on the nearby Great White Throne—that was a seat for a deity—but would instead reverently perch on a nearby footstool to pay their obeisance. Hence "Angels Landing" and what is today one of the most popular and exciting hikes in the National Park.

The name "Angels Landing" was obviously much more appealing and memorable to visitors than the original name of the feature.

Fisher is also credited with giving several other Zion landmarks the "heavenly" names that persist to this day. Among them is the "Three Patriarchs" (Abraham, Isaac and Jacob).

V

Utah Disasters Cloaked in History

38

WHEN SALT LAKE LITERALLY EXPLODED

It was the General Conference of the Church of Jesus Christ of Latter-day Saints that started off with a big bang. On April 5, 1876, at 4:48 p.m., the powder magazines at Arsenal Hill (west of where today's Utah State Capitol stands and just below today's DUP Pioneer Museum) exploded with a fury of forty tons of gunpowder that *Deseret News* reports compared with the devil himself.

A trio of explosions rocked the city the afternoon before the semiannual four-day conference started. The Arsenal, the only building then on Salt Lake City's northwest bench, was leveled. The following day's headline in the *Deseret News* was: "Terrible Disaster. Terrific Explosion of Forty Tons of Giant, Hercules, Blasting and Other Powder. Four Persons Killed Instantly and Others Injured. Great Damage to Property."

The raining debris covered a two-mile radius. The explosions were felt in shaking buildings as far north as Kaysville. Four different gunpowder magazines exploded, creating four separate bombs of debris.

Some people shouted, "A volcano!," and others yelled, "An earthquake!," as an immense mass of flame shot heavenward. One reporter described the calamity as an eruption with "a column of smoke and debris as grand as Vesuvius ever belched forth."

Hundreds of people were lying on the ground, women and children screamed and many men turned pale, according to *Deseret News* reports. Some ran toward the explosion, others away. Many animals bolted from wagons, frightened by the loud noise.

A panoramic view of Salt Lake City, probably in the 1870s. *Courtesy of Utah State Historical Society.*

Two young men, identified as Frank Hill and Charles Richardson, both eighteen, were near the building at the time of the explosion. They had been tending cattle on the hill earlier in the day and were known to have been shooting a rifle at birds. They were killed instantly by the explosion. The men were suspected of causing the explosion when a burning paper wad from their shotgun ignited some loose gunpowder.

No specific blame for the explosion was assigned, but a jury requested additional precautions for any other explosives kept in the city.

Vandals had previously shot through the Arsenal's main iron doors with guns for sport and target practice. The building was made of rock, with a tin roof, but a thicker iron door was added after repeated vandalism.

Also killed were Mary Jane Van Natta, struck on the head by a rock as she was pumping water outside. James Raddon Jr., five, died when he was struck in the chest by a rock while playing outside. Another woman was said to have died from fright after the explosion.

Broken glass created the biggest problem. Hardly any Main Street business or nearby Church meetinghouse had an unbroken window left. The walls of the Twentieth Ward schoolhouse were badly damaged. There were no reports of damage to the Salt Lake Temple, under construction at the time, but it was likely only in the first-story stage.

Several merchants were charged with selling glass at twice the usual price in the days after the explosion.

A large boulder went through the mayor's roof and two floors of his new home. A flying rock took away part of the ear of a son of D.P. Kimball.

Several residents reported moving babies or children from rooms that were soon thereafter heavily hit by raining debris. Several dozen boys playing baseball to the west of the armory were knocked to the ground twice by the explosions and found shelter to avoid the biggest shower of debris.

President Brigham Young's flour mill, a half mile away up City Creek, was destroyed, as were the covers for the city waterworks and the adjacent building near City Creek. One of President Young's daughters, sitting near a window on South Temple, suffered a head wound from shattering glass.

One Civil War veteran said after the explosion that he saw less damage in Fredericksburg after a month of cannon bombardment than he did following the explosion. The *Deseret News* reported two days after the explosion:

> *The Prince of the Power of the Air had a roisterly time on Wednesday afternoon.....Not many of our citizens, previously, had any realizing idea of the immense reserve force stored up in a few grains of charcoal, and nitre and Sulphur....The explosion has been the main topic of conversation in the city ever since and will be more or less for future days to come. Years in the future, the time of it will be referenced to as an era, whence and with which the happenings of other events will be calculated and compared.*

Other newspapers made the disaster sound even worse. For example, one headline read: "Nearly every house in Salt Lake more or less wrecked." Other stories also spoke of 200-pound boulders, although the largest confirmed boulder of debris to hit downtown was 115 pounds—a rock that struck the Theatre Saloon on 100 South.

Still, the *Deseret News* reported every building within a radius of one and a half to two miles of the explosion sustained some sort of damage. Apparently, no general conference talks made reference to the disaster, or at least nothing was recorded by conference reporters.

The Arsenal building was reduced to craters. It was privately owned by the DuPont Company and had cost $26,000 to construct. According to some sources, the Arsenal was at the top of Main Street, about two blocks north of Temple Square and approximately near today's Daughters of the Utah Pioneers Building at 300 North Main. But photographs taken in the Arsenal area after the explosion make it more likely that the building was at about 200 North Main. The Arsenal was never rebuilt.

The area surrounding Arsenal Hill in the 1860s and 1870s consisted of bare, open fields. The area was vacant, probably because not until the late 1880s was a year-round water supply secured for the area.

This, of course, was long before the area came to be known as Capitol Hill. The entire plateau between Ensign Peak and Temple Square was originally called Prospect Hill. Then, when the Arsenal was placed there, probably in the early 1860s, it became Arsenal Hill.

Not until February 28, 1888, did Elder Heber J. Grant propose that the Salt Lake City municipality donate twenty acres of the former Arsenal Hill property for a future capitol building site. The actual donation took place on March 1 of that year. The Utah State Capitol was slow in coming and wasn't started until 1913 and completed in 1915.

39

WHEN ALTA WAS A SYNONYM
FOR AVALANCHE

The most dangerous place to live in Utah during the late nineteenth century was undoubtedly Alta.

The following is a sample of newspaper headlines from avalanche disasters in the historic mining town of Alta: "Unhappy Alta," "The Awful Avalanche," "Terrible Tragedy," "Latest Alta Horror," "Alta Is Swept Away," "More Snowslides—Six Persons Killed at Alta," "Terrible Snow-Slide in Cottonwood" and "Another Horror." Indeed, one newspaper story called Alta "home of the avalanche."

From 1872 to 1927, at least eighty-seven people were killed in fourteen different avalanches at Alta, according to research from DigitalNewspapers. org. (The primary reason that avalanche deaths in Alta dropped after 1927 was that the price of silver plummeted in 1927, after which this silver-mining town was all but abandoned until the skiing era arrived.)

Yes, avalanches occurred in other Wasatch Mountain locations during that era. For example, the most deadly single avalanche, on February 27, 1926, in Bingham Canyon killed forty people. Other slides at Bingham killed at least three others in earlier years. But Alta had the most slides; several times, the entire town was swept away.

Many animals also perished in these slides, usually mules and horses.

The *Deseret News* of March 12, 1884, reported the following: "Avalanche at Alta. Twelve people killed at New Emma Mine. The awful news reached this city yesterday of a fatal snow-slide near Alta, Little Cottonwood Canyon, in which twelve persons, nine men, two women and a boy perished."

A large avalanche at Alta, as shown in an undated photograph. *Courtesy of Utah State Historical Society.*

On February 18, 1885, the paper reported a snowslide that killed sixteen people: "The Alta avalanche. Further particulars of the sad catastrophe.... The avalanche covered more ground than any before known in that vicinity, and its effects were far more disastrous....Of the many buildings in the main part of town, only seven were left standing."

Why did people keep living in the area and working the mines in Alta despite one disaster after another? A *Salt Lake Herald* story from February 15, 1885, right after the slide that killed sixteen people, may have the best answers. It referred to the avalanche as "the same old story" and stated:

> *The poor men and women who have been ruthlessly stricken down were not in Alta because they preferred the isolation, the discomforts and dangers of the snow-bound camp to the pleasure and safety of city homes; they were there for the same reason which induces the Swiss peasant to brave the terrors of winters in the Alps...they were there for the bread that they must have....We can honor them, for they were heroes and heroines, for they had the courage to fight nature's battle against nature's threatenings.*

Avalanches have historically been one of the biggest natural killers in Utah. But the Utah Avalanche Center didn't begin recording accidents until the post-mining decades, beginning with 1940. (The first avalanche death by a skier at Alta was in January 1941.)

Even today, avalanches are a hallmark of Little Cottonwood Canyon, the home of Alta and Snowbird ski resorts. Highway 210 heads up Little Cottonwood Canyon and is one of the most avalanche-prone roads in the world. That's because the thirteen-and-six-tenths-mile-long highway in the canyon crosses through sixty-four different avalanche paths.

Artillery is regularly used in the canyon to keep it avalanche-free today. In fact, using such explosives to control avalanches saw its first worldwide usage in Little Cottonwood Canyon in the 1940s.

40

WHEN PARK CITY LAID IN ASHES

I t was likely the largest city fire ever in Utah.

"Destroyed!; [Park] City Practically Wiped Out; A Raging Conflagration; Scene of Ruin and Despair," was a *Deseret News* headline on June 20, 1898. A fire on Sunday, June 19, 1898, just after 4:00 a.m., all but destroyed the prosperous mining town. No lives were lost, but there were many narrow escapes, and many animals were killed.

"Park City, Utah's proud and prosperous mining camp, has practically been wiped out of existence, being visited yesterday by the most disastrous conflagration in the history of Utah," the *Deseret News* reported. "It may be that the city will be rebuilt and rise again from the ruins that now cover the canyon where it once stood, but it will be years before it can fully recover— if recovery is at all possible under the circumstances—from the terrible visitation. The loss, it is conservatively estimated, will aggregate more than a million dollars. The actual insurance will not reach much more than a tenth of that amount."

The cause of the fire, also described as a "fiery furnace," was never determined. The speculation was that it began in the kitchen of the American Hotel. But the proprietor, Harry Freeman, believed that an oil lamp had been dropped in a room or simply that a candle had been left unattended.

The *Salt Lake Herald* declared on June 20, 1898: "Park City laid in ashes yesterday. Great cap suffers a loss of over half a million dollars. Insurance will not be much over one hundred thousand." The story cited the historic town's bad luck. First, it had suffered from the economic downturn of 1893.

Modern Main Street in Park City is pictured in 2007. It looks nothing like the original downtown Park City. *Author photo.*

Then the main Park City bank failed, followed by a reduction in the wages of miners and mill workers. And finally, the giant fire struck the town. The story referred to the fire as "demon flame" and stated that "the hope for the future is small."

The four existing fire hoses had little effect on the blaze. Buildings were soon dynamited, but all this did was slow the fire, not stop it. Firemen came from Coalville, Salt Lake and Ogden, mostly by train. But they did not arrive until midmorning, when it was too late to do much but watch. It was not until noon that the fire was contained.

In the end, at least 120 businesses and 140 homes were wiped out—some 75 percent of the town. At least five hundred people were left homeless.

A January 7, 1996 story in the *Deseret News* by Twila Van Leer stated that the disastrous fire made national headlines and even superseded the Spanish-American War as the top story in some U.S. papers.

What happened after the fire? The majority of the residents remained and rebuilt. (There had been a much smaller downtown Park City fire in 1890.) Salt Lake City gave $2,500.00 to Park City's rebuilding efforts. The

City of Mount Pleasant gave $102.40, and many Utahns donated or helped in the rebuilding effort.

Thirty-four miners were killed in a 1902 explosion at a Park City mine—another tragedy for the town.

Ultimately, Park City's mining prospects diminished, and the town suffered a big downturn. But thanks to skiing and the annual Sundance Film Festival, the town reinvented itself as a tourist mecca by the 1980s and 1990s. Park City was also famed worldwide during the 2002 Winter Olympics.

Although Park City, like Moab, is often pegged as a "Gentile" or largely non-Mormon town, its name originated from an LDS Church apostle, Parley P. Pratt. Elder Pratt built a toll road through Parley's Canyon. Settlers at the top of the road called it "Parley's Park City." But by the early twentieth century, the name had been shortened to Park City.

WHEN A WALL OF WATER HIT MANTI

U tah was plagued by summer cloudbursts and flooding in the early twentieth century. Mostly caused by overgrazing, the most infamous of such floods struck Willard and Farmington in the early 1920s. But a summer flood several decades earlier, in 1899, devastated Manti, Utah.

The *Times-News* of Nephi, Utah, reported on July 14, 1899: "A wall of water. The City of Manti swept by a cloudburst. Streets turned into a

The stream in Manti Canyon, as shown in the spring of 2021. A flash flood came from here in July 1899. *Author photo*.

raging river. Thousands of dollars of damage done—No lives are lost." The flood, with overgrazing by sheep as a contributing factor, roared out of Manti Canyon, on the city's east side, and made the town look like the bed of a river.

"At about 6:45 [p.m.] some men came riding down from the canyon, shouting that a flood was coming, but the people were loth to believe the report," the newspaper stated. "In an incredible short time after the warning a wall of water about eight or ten feet high came rushing down the creek carrying with it an immense quantity of logs, stumps and other debris."

Some logs jammed under a bridge, forming a dam and directing much of the water into town. Cellars were filled with mud, and crops were damaged. It was estimated that up to $60,000 damage was done to the town. A mass meeting of residents was called to start a cleanup effort.

42

WHEN CLOUDBURSTS SCOURED
THE CANYONS

Cloudburst Death Toll Mounts, Mangled Bodies Found in Debris; Scouts Victims" was an August 14, 1923 headline in the *Ogden Standard-Examiner*. These floods struck Willard, Farmington and Centerville, causing hundreds of thousands of dollars in property damage and killing eight people. Two fatalities occurred below Willard Canyon, and six came in or around Farmington Canyon.

Floods from a gigantic summer cloudburst damaged a Centerville home in 1923. *Courtesy of Utah State Historical Society*.

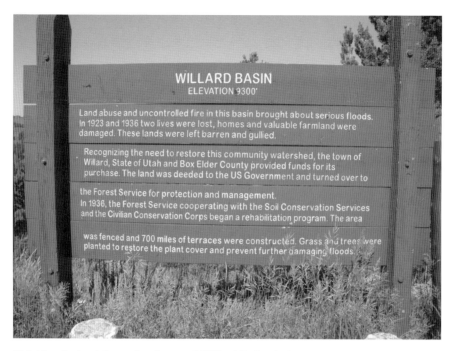

This historic sign is located at the top of Willard Basin. *Author photo*.

Crops in the wide area were ruined, and the main highway was blocked by up to six feet of mud in Willard and Farmington.

Flood crests in Farmington Canyon were observed to be seventy-five to one hundred feet high and two hundred feet across. Patrons at Lagoon had to be rescued from trees or roofs, where they had fled from the rising waters. The town of Willard lost all electrical power and communications, as did most of Farmington.

A.L. Glasmann, editor of the *Standard*, rushed to Willard after hearing of the disaster and worked throughout the night helping people. "The district is a picture of desolation," he said. The *Standard* set up a relief fund and helped raised thousands of dollars for flood victims.

Much of the devastation resulted from overgrazing in the Wasatch Mountains. In the 1930s, government programs created reservoirs, terraces and flood basins above Willard and from Farmington to Centerville in the mountains to help prevent future disasters.

43

RECALLING THE INFAMOUS UTAH WINTER OF 1948–49

L ooking back to the frigid and snowy winter of 1948–49 makes more recent winters look pretty tame—even the snowy winter of 2022–23. Some old-timers, as well as historical records, indicate that the winter of 1948–49 was likely the worst recorded winter period in northern Utah since the 1800s. Take Ogden City, for example. On January 26, 1949, Ogden shivered with its coldest recorded temperature: sixteen degrees below zero.

But low temperatures are only part of this chilling story. The winter of 1948–9 had a frightful combination of bone-chilling temperatures, heavy snowfall, howling winds and even inversions.

The National Weather Service ranks that winter as the fourth-worst weather event for Utah in the twentieth century. It described the season in this way: "Utah's most severe winter since 1899....It was the coldest winter on record, with record amounts of seasonal snowfall....Nearly a 25 percent loss in some livestock herds reported. Many fruit trees were killed. Wildlife struggled for existence. Tourist trade reached an all-time low, and 10 people died from exposure."

The Utah State Division of History refers to it as "1948's Unforgettable Winter" and includes reports from areas of the Wasatch Front where the snow piles and drifts were as high as the telephone wires. Driving down the road was like traveling through a tunnel.

Utah winters of the mid-1980s and 1993 were infamous for heavy snowfalls, but they lacked subzero temperatures and howling winds, as did

State Street in Salt Lake City, looking north, is shown in the horrendous winter of 1948–49. *Courtesy of Utah State Historical Society.*

the winter of 2022–23. For example, on January 23 and January 24, 1949, there were twenty-three inches of snow at the Salt Lake Airport, the third-greatest amount on record. Then, on January 25, the temperature dipped to seven degrees below zero. The high never topped eight degrees above zero.

Anyone born before the start of World War II may be able to recall how terrible that winter was.

The journal of Venice Flygare, of Ogden, my late mother-in-law, includes her description of that significant winter: "It was a very hard winter, lots of snow," she wrote. "There was very seldom a snowplow that went along our street and no garbage pickup or mail delivery. There were many nights when we could park our car on 30th Street and walk the half block to our house [at 1328 Walcott Street]."

Another relative, Milas Erastus Wakefield, wrote about that winter with a one-line entry: "1949 was a very hard winter, lots of snow and cold weather."

Brent K. Thurgood of Hooper also recalled that awful winter: "I remember it well, as I was 5 years old and living in Ogden at the time, in Bonneville Park, a government subdivision. The road to the North of our house was a narrow one-way road but the snow plowed and blown off of it created a snow bank on both sides about 12–15 feet high."

He continued: "We had to dig a tunnel through to get to our house. I remember climbing to the top and sliding down with and without a sleigh. I also remember the black smog over Ogden. My house was on Quincy Avenue and you could see the black smoke and steam from the trains coming into and leaving the train depot. The black soot would fall on the snow each night. My mother hung our laundry out to dry and the clothes were covered with soot also."

Margaret Brough of Kaysville also recalled that icy winter with a lot of detail. "I lived in West Jordan during that time and I was a Sophomore at Jordan High School," Brough recalled.

The Bingham Highway from Redwood Road up to the copper mine was snowed in. We had a lot of snow and then the winds would blow snow drifts into the roads. The Bingham High way was closed for (it seems like) about 6 weeks. All the area between West Jordan and Bingham was mostly dry farms. The people did not have a way to get to the store for supplies or for feed for their animals. I remember someone took the body of a small airplane and built things that looked like pontoons on the bottom and he would fly from house to house to get orders for food, and feed for the animals and deliver it. Airport Number 2 was in operation at the time and I am sure this guy operated out of there.

She continued:

We lived down a lane and one night as my father was coming home, the truck got stuck half way down the lane. My father walked home and by morning the truck was completely covered. For weeks we would walk down the lane to catch the school bus and it seemed like that truck was completely covered and you did not know where the truck was until spring. Suddenly the top of the truck became visible and it was still quite a few days before my father was able to get the truck home.

When the Bingham highway was opened it was done by a rotary plow. The plow would pile snow up on the snow that was already taller than the snowplow. We had a neighbor who would take the bus to 7800 South and Redwood Road and then he would walk a mile up the Bingham Highway to his house. The first night that the Bingham Highway was unplowed, he was walking on the top of the snow piled up by the side of the road.

He was about 6-feet-2 and he bumped into the cross bar on the top of the light pole and knocked himself out. It was a few days after this happened that trucks began to haul some of the snow away.

Brough noted this startling fact:

Jordan High School was closed down for three or four days right around the 20th of January until we could get the roads open for the buses to operate. It was cold and the wind did blow a lot. I have pictures around our yard where the piles of snow were twice as tall as a 5-foot-2 girl would be standing. It was quite a feat. That was the coldest winter I have ever lived through.

The Wasatch Front was stuck in a temperature inversion for long periods that winter. In an era when burning coal was the most common source of heating, air pollution levels must have been off the scale.

December 1948 produced thirty-nine inches of snow at Salt Lake Airport. There were only seven days that month lacking snowfall. Plus, there were just eight snowless days in January 1949 and nine in February. To make it even worse, it snowed on eleven of the thirty-one days in March 1949. December in Salt Lake City boasted two subzero temperature days; January had thirteen and February four. (Historically, the city averages only three days of zero degrees or below a year.) Ogden and points north of Salt Lake likely were as cold or colder than Salt Lake was.

Winds were also a curse that winter. With the extra cold temperatures, the snow was light, and it didn't take much wind to create dangerous drifts. On February 7, 1949, ten inches of snow were recorded at the airport, followed by near-hurricane-force winds. The blowing snow closed schools in the Davis and Weber school districts.

Milk and egg production dropped substantially. "Operation Haylift" used aircraft to drop food to struggling livestock in rural areas.

A photo collection at the University of Utah has this caption attached to an image of a winter snow pile in central Utah: "The winter of 1948–49 was unforgettable. Snow was on the ground for 5 months. The snow which had been plowed to the sides of the road became so high that it had to be hauled off in trucks."

Coal supplies ran low in Utah that winter. During portions of February, all roads north of Brigham City were closed. Trains were even snowed in. A snowslide buried a train in Cache County and killed three railroad workers.

Layton City work crews are shown hauling extra snow away during the record winter of 1948–49. *Courtesy of Heritage Museum of Layton.*

In parts of Wyoming, drastic methods were used: Flamethrowers cleared the Union Pacific tracks in February 1949.

Idaho also had a severe winter that season. February 4–February 11, 1949, was likely Idaho's worst ever winter blast. Three snowplows and their drivers were stranded overnight between Pocatello and American Falls. Many road repairs were required in the spring.

So, maybe all those trite-sounding tales from seniors about trudging through deep snow to school in their youth were not all exaggerated after all.

44

UTAH'S HOLIDAY RAILROAD
DISASTER

New Year's Eve is usually the holiday for hopeful futures and new beginnings. But the last holiday of the year in 1944 ended with tragedy and the state's worst train disaster.

"Pacific Limited Crash Claims 48 Lives," was a January 1, 1945 headline in the *Standard-Examiner*. The somber headlines in the *Standard* that day were: "Reporter Finds Tragic Horror at Wreck Scene," "Wreck Reminded Me of War, Says Train Crash Victim" and "Screams, Moans Rend the Air at Wreck Scene."

A pair of westbound trains crashed shortly after 6:00 a.m. on December 31, 1944, near Promontory Point, or about eighteen miles west of Ogden, on the Lucin Cutoff.

Besides the forty-eight fatalities, another seventy-nine people were reported injured in the crash. Among the fatalities were twenty-nine military personnel and nine railroad workers. This was the worst rail disaster in the Intermountain area and the nation's worst railroad crash of 1944.

By January 5, 1945, the death toll from the wreck had risen to fifty. The disaster came to be known as the Bagley Train Wreck or the Great Salt Lake Wreck.

The accident happened in thick fog when a mail express train failed to slow down for a caution signal and smashed at full speed, sixty miles per hour, into the rear of the Pullman car of a passenger train, which had slowed to eighteen miles per hour for a freight train ahead with mechanical

Two passenger trains crashed on December 31, 1944, killing forty-eight people, along the Southern Pacific line. *Courtesy of Utah State Historical Society.*

problems. (In some other accounts, the engineer of the mail train may have suffered a heart attack and died seconds before the crash.)

Seven of the railcars were hurled off the wooden lake trestle and into the Great Salt Lake's mud and shallow, briny waters. The wreck scene stretched for a half mile.

Fortunately, there were two medical cars in the passenger train. U.S. Army Medical Corps members helped the injured; otherwise, help had to wait until arrival by rail from Ogden.

45

OGDEN'S LEGENDARY TRAIN ROBBERY MYSTERY

T he Golden Spike in Utah completed the transcontinental railroad on May 10, 1869. The Ogden area's most dastardly train robbery actually happened almost forty-two years later, more recently than depicted in most Hollywood versions of the Wild West, on January 2, 1911.

According to a headline in the January 3 *Ogden Standard-Examiner*, "Train Held Up, One Man Killed and Passengers Robbed Just West of Ogden." This may have been one of the last of the area's big train robberies and was referred to at the time as "the most daring train robbery ever planned and executed in the west."

Thieves robbed the Overland Limited at Reese, about nine miles west of Ogden. Besides the robbery, the two masked men with short-barreled rifles shot and killed a porter and wounded another porter. The shootings appeared racially motivated. The robbery happened shortly before midnight, and word of the crime reached Ogden about two hours later.

The men had tried to steal the engine of the train in order to reach Ogden but were thwarted by a freight train following the Limited. They robbed two girls in Warren en route to Ogden and were believed to be somewhere in town. The men appeared to have intricate knowledge of the operation of the railroad. Their only shortcoming was in failing to account for a train following their train.

Posses set out in every direction the day after the robbery but failed to find a trace of the bandits. The alleged bandits, W. Lewis, thirty-nine, and Peter

This historic photograph, taken on May 22, 1911, shows Bryan O'Hara and Victor Clore with two sheriff's deputies as they were released from jail. *Courtesy of Ogden City.*

Murphy, thirty-seven, were caught eleven days later sleeping in an Ogden lodging house at 2417 Grant Avenue.

The headline in the January 14, 1911 *Standard* read, "Holdups Make No Effort to Resist Officers." One of the men captured immediately held out his wrists to be handcuffed. A "great crowd was attracted to the scene of the arrest." The men's landlady said they had been gambling with their new wealth. Two other men, who acted as fences for the thieves, were also arrested.

Police reported that they believed the same two men had held up the Oregon Short Line near Ogden in the summer of 1910 and had also robbed an Ogden pawn shop. "All afternoon the [Ogden] police station was besieged by persons desiring to catch some sight of the bandits," the *Standard* reported. But that wasn't the end of the story. Soon, the police released Murphy and kept Lewis, but they decided that Thomas O'Dell was the other culprit, according to the *Standard-Examiner* of January 16, 1911.

But within days, those two suspects had been released for lack of evidence. "Suspects Are to Leave the Jail," was the *Standard*'s January 23 headline.

Next, the Weber County Sheriff's Office received tips and extradited Bryan O'Hara and Victor Clore from Michigan as prime suspects. But on May 22, 1911, those two men were also released because of a lack of sufficient evidence. No robbers were ever found for that great crime. It remains an unsolved mystery to this day.

A historic photograph taken on May 22, 1911, shows Bryan O'Hara and Victor Clore with two sheriff's deputies as they were released from jail after a district judge cited a lack of evidence.

In the aftermath of the train robbery, as indicated by a headline in the *Standard* on January 7, "Trains Are to Carry Guards." All Harrison Company passenger trains were to include heavily armed guards to prevent future robberies.

Yet the 1911 train robbery wasn't the last for the Ogden area. Smaller railroad thefts occasionally still took place. For example, in March 1916, a "Gentleman robber," whose "commands were mild in good language," stole mail off a train in Roy. The lone robber missed taking the local mailbag and walked off with two out-of-state bags, according to a March 29 *Standard* report. There was no report indicating that the robber was ever caught.

VI

The Dark Side of Utah's National Parks

What follows is a sampling of primarily hiking and climbing accidents in Utah's five national parks, current through the first quarter of 2023.

ACCIDENTS IN
ARCHES NATIONAL PARK

May 29, 1950, Landscape Arch: Frederich Semisch, nineteen, of New York City, fell some four hundred feet to his death attempting to climb one of the park's largest arches. He lost his footing climbing an arch that some believe has never been successfully mounted. Climbing the arch involves navigating a one-hundred-foot narrow knife-edge, and the arch is only six feet in diameter at certain points. A photographer saw Semisch scream and then fall.

September 14, 1969, Navajo Arch: Andrea Hernandez of Miami, Florida, suffered a hand injury when a boulder fell on it while she was hiking off a trail near the arch. She required surgery on her hand.

March 11, 1972, Delicate Arch: Zaner Edwin Miller, forty-three, of Spokane, Washington, died of an apparent heart attack at the base of the arch.

April 1972, various locations: Four different accidents were reported during the same busy spring week. March 29: Raymond W. France of California fell 30 feet off a fin near Double O Arch and suffered a broken hand and pelvis. March 31: John Dvorozniak, twenty-three, from Colorado, slid 30 feet down a rock fin, stopping short of another 125-foot cliff. He suffered minor injuries. April 1: Strub Bateman, seventeen, of Salt Lake City, sprained an ankle scrambling around Devil's Garden. April 2: Peter Greenwald of Roy sustained a broken leg and pelvis fractures when he was struck by a vehicle while riding his motorcycle in the park.

Arches National Park, probably shown in the 1940s, when climbing atop arches was not a rare occurrence. *Courtesy of Utah State Historical Society.*

A pair of women enjoys the scenery of Arches National Park, probably in the early 1950s. *Courtesy of Utah State Historical Society.*

August 7, 1977, Devil's Garden: David Shapiro, twenty-three, of Chicago, Illinois, had to be rescued after falling 40 feet while attempting to cross a sandstone ridge. Only another ledge prevented him from falling another 250 feet to the canyon floor. He suffered a head injury. His extraction was one of the most complicated in early park history. Rescue equipment had to be carried up and across a narrow, 300-foot-high fin and then lowered 40 feet to reach the injured man.

November 29, 2019, Delicate Arch: Toshiaki Amimoto, sixty-five, and Etoko Amimoto, sixty, both of Torrance, California, died in falls off the arch. The area was slick and wet at the time of the accidents.

October 1, 2022: Thirty-three-year-old Ekaterina Yaroslavna Ksenjek of Arlington, Virginia, was found dead in Devils Garden. The cause of death is unknown.

February 24, 2023: A seventy-one-year-old man from Massachusetts collapsed and died on a trail in Arches Park.

March 6, 2023: A fifty-six-year-old man collapsed and died on the Devils Garden Trail in Arches.

MISHAPS IN BRYCE CANYON NATIONAL PARK

Octuber 24, 1947, canyon rim: Fifty-two passengers died near the rim of Bryce Canyon when their United Airlines DC-6 exploded. (This airplane accident is included, as it involves by far the greatest number of deaths in one day in a Utah national park.)

April 22, 1954, Fairview Point: Emma Webner, a sixty-one-year-old tourist, died in a ninety-eight-foot fall at Fairview Point. It took crews three hours to recover her body.

June 12, 1979, Paria View Overlook: Amandinc Delavy, two, died when she slipped through the lower rail of a fence, lost her balance and fell 125 feet down.

December 14, 1990, Queen's Garden Trail: A twenty-one-year-old Cedar City, Utah man was hiking in the dark when he stepped off the trail and slid down a thirty-five-foot frozen slope. His two companions rushed back to their vehicle and were able to improvise with jackets, pants and tire chains in twenty-degree weather to fashion a successful rescue line and pull the man up.

February 14, 1991, Bryce Point: Craig Olsen, thirteen, of Magna, died from a three-hundred-foot fall. He was attempting to retrieve a dropped camera from a small ledge when he lost his footing.

June 28, 1991, Inspiration Point: A tourist from France scrambled sixty feet below the rim for a picture. He soon fell fifteen feet when the outcropping he was standing on collapsed. He was able to hang on to avoid an additional one-hundred-foot fall until rangers used a winch to rescue him.

Visitors getting too close to the rim is a frequent danger at Bryce Canyon National Park. *Author photo*.

September 24, 1992, Inspiration Point: A California woman with memory problems became separated from her sixty-six-year-old mother and became lost overnight. Twenty searchers and a helicopter located the woman two miles from where she had been last seen. Despite freezing temperatures, she suffered only from dehydration.

December 8, 1994, Sunrise Point: Joseph Tall, sixty-six, of Sequim, Washington, died in a fall at Bryce. He was reported missing, and his body was found later below the rim.

July 20, 1995, Inspiration Point: Linda Ann Munnerlyn, thirty-six, of Denver, Colorado, died from a three-hundred-foot fall while gathering flowers along the rim. At the time, she was only the fourth visitor to die in a fall at Bryce.

March 28, 2000, canyon rim: A twenty-one-year-old man was rescued after he slipped and was stranded on a ledge twenty-five feet below the rim. The victim said that he'd been "skiing" down the loose gravel along the rim when he slipped and fell. He was uninjured.

September 16, 2003, Navajo Loop Trail: A fifty-nine-year-old man from the United Kingdom died from a head injury after falling down a twenty-

A throng of visitors hikes down the north side of the Navajo Trail at Bryce Canyon in the 1930s. *Courtesy of Utah State Historical Society.*

foot slope. A nearby doctor from France was able to respond within a minute, but the man was unresponsive.

October 11, 2003, Queen's Garden Trail: A forty-nine-year-old man from Michigan died in a fall inside Bryce Canyon. He had walked onto to a narrow fin and attempted to climb a rock formation when he slipped out of sight. His was the second falling fatality in the park during 2003.

May 29, 2010, Peek-a-Boo Trail: A woman with a serious leg fracture had to be rescued by helicopter from below the rim.

November 7, 2012, Under-the-Rim Trail: A forty-eight-year-old Maryland woman was reported missing and had to be rescued. The woman had hiked more than ten miles over two days clad only in a T-shirt and shorts and with minimal water and food. Temperatures dropped into the thirties at night. She had built a shelter to survive the cold night and left four SOS messages for rescuers. She was found after twenty-nine hours.

January 11, 2014, Riggs Spring Loop: Two Utah women had to be rescued after they became lost in the park's snowy backcountry. They had lost the trail in snow up to three feet deep. They eventually made a fire but had to be located with a helicopter assist. They had warm clothing but had not taken their snowshoes, a GPS device, a compass or maps into the canyon.

March 22, 2014, Hat Shop Trail: A group of hikers had to be rescued after they became lost and were ill-prepared to spend the night in cold weather. A helicopter from Page, Arizona, helped locate them.

July 26, 2014, Peek-a-Boo Trail: A trail rider had to extracted by helicopter after the mule he was riding threw him off during a guided tour. He was seriously injured. The accident happened two and a half miles from the nearest trailhead.

January 30, 2019, below the rim: Two lost California hikers had to be rescued during extreme winter conditions. They were not well prepared to hike in cold weather.

May 3, 2019: Park rangers rescued a man who had been lost below the rim for four days without food or water. The man had planned a two-hour hike in Swamp Canyon but became lost. He was suffering from dehydration and had some bruises. A helicopter was used to assist in his rescue.

October 23, 2020, Under-the-Rim Trail: A missing hiker was rescued after what was supposed to be a four-hour loop hike until he became lost. He was found the following day, dehydrated.

Note: Lightning strikes during storms are a significant danger, especially to tourists strolling along the Bryce Canyon rim. Between 1989 and 2023, five visitors have been injured by lightning strikes and another two have died.

48

CALAMITIES IN CANYONLANDS NATIONAL PARK

Augb ugust 7, 1972, Island in the Sky: Howard Sard, seventeen, of New York City, slid 175 feet on a slickrock ridge. He was rendered unconscious but had no broken bones ("Boy Injured in Canyonlands," *Times Independent* (Moab, UT), August 10, 1972).

February 21, 1977, Needles area: Brett Lewis, a University of Utah student, fell and suffered a broken leg in a park accident. One of his three companions contacted rangers. The accident happened two and a half miles from the nearest jeep road, around Druid Arch ("Injured in Canyonlands," *Times Independent*, February 24, 1977).

March 18, 1978, Monument Basin: Bob Dowdcy, thirty-six, of Salt Lake City, was hurt when he fell twenty feet, injuring his leg. His hiking companion was unable to reach him, but she lowered him food and his sleeping bag. She contacted rangers the next morning. He was rescued despite the difficult terrain ("Hiker Hurt in Fall in Canyonlands," *Times Independent*, March 23, 1978).

June 5, 1990, Syncline Loop Trail: A forty-three-year-old Flagstaff, Arizona woman became lost while hiking far ahead of her companion. A helicopter spotted her signal fire.

October 16, 1991, White Rim overlook: A thirty-three-year-old Savannah, Georgia woman fell to her death. Her husband heard her scream and fall. Her body was recovered by helicopter.

August 12, 1992, Elephant Canyon: A thirty-seven-year-old Columbus, Ohio woman was hiking by herself when she became lost. She was found the next day uninjured.

Angel Arch is located in a remote southern section of Canyonlands National Park. *Courtesy of Utah State Historical Society.*

November 29, 1992, Big Springs Canyon: A fifty-one-year-old man from Switzerland died in a seventy-foot fall off a snow-covered slickrock dome.

May 29 and June 3, 1993: Park rangers had to recover the bodies of three men who drowned in the Green and Colorado Rivers.

August 2, 1995, Island in the Sky: A forty-year-old man from Key West, Florida, became lost. He hiked forty-six miles over twenty-four hours in temperatures above one hundred degrees at times. Certain that he was going to die, he penned a farewell letter. He was discovered by a park road maintenance crew.

September 27, 1997, Colorado River: A forty-year-old South Jordan, Utah man drowned in a noncommercial rafting accident in Cataract Canyon.

November 8, 1997, Mat Martin Point: A group of five young adults became stranded on a four-hundred-foot cliff above the Colorado River, thirteen miles north of Moab. Passing motorists heard their cries for help and contacted authorities.

November 14, 1998, Needles area: The body of a forty-one-year-old Telluride, Colorado man was found. He had fallen about thirty feet off the "The Naked and Dead" climbing route.

March 13, 2000, Needles District: A twenty-eight-year-old Texas man died in a long fall. His body had to be extracted by helicopter.

August 1, 2000, Moab area: A thirteen-year-old boy from Woodstock, Illinois, went missing while mountain biking. Some one hundred people searched for him. The boy's body was found four days later about two and a half miles from his abandoned bicycle. Daytime temperatures reached 110 degrees during the search.

December 30, 2000, Mineral Point: A twenty-four-year-old woman from Texas had to be rescued after a BASE jumping accident. Her chute became tangled on significantly protruding rock about 230 feet from the ground and 270 feet from the top. She was rescued and raised to the cliff top by rangers.

February 9, 2001, Indian Creek Canyon: A twenty-nine-year-old woman fell ninety feet to her death while solo climbing. Friends of the climber saw her fall and contacted rangers.

April 24, 2001, White Rim Road: A forty-four-year-old Colorado man died when he pedaled his mountain bike into a boulder adjacent to a curve.

October 13, 2002, Shafer Canyon: A twenty-year-old University of Colorado student died in a five-hundred-foot fall from the west rim of the Middle Fork of the canyon. No one saw the man fall, but friends searched for him and contacted rangers.

April 26, 2003, Blue John Canyon: This is the infamous self-rescue of a twenty-seven-year-old Aspen, Colorado man, Aaron Ralston. After five days of being trapped, he had to resort to an extreme action or die. He had to amputate his right arm to escape from being pinned by a boulder in a remote area. The eight-hundred-pound boulder had shifted and trapped the man in a standing position during a descent. After applying a tourniquet, he was able to rappel to the canyon floor and then hike out the more popular Horseshoe Canyon, where he was found by a helicopter. His arm was later recovered by authorities.

April 28, 2003, Island in the Sky: A sixty-nine-year-old woman fell thirty feet and suffered a fractured arm and a head injury. The husband dragged her into the shade and hiked a mile to a road and flagged a vehicle down for help.

April 9, 2004, Big Springs overlook: A fifty-four-year-old Colorado woman fell 120 feet to her death from the overlook. The death was ruled accidental.

November 2, 2005, White Rim Road: A thirty-seven-year-old Colorado man fell off a forty-foot cliff. Alcohol consumption was considered a factor in the fall.

April 30, 2007, Buck Mesa: A group of stranded hikers had to be rescued about five hundred feet above the canyon floor. They had become lost and unable to proceed. They thought they were going to die, given their lack of water and the high temperatures. A park maintenance worker saw the stranded men, and a helicopter aided their rescue.

June 17, 2008, Orange Cliffs: A seventy-three-year-old Virginia man was found dead, likely from in a seventy-foot fall from the overlook. He probably died several days earlier. His abandoned vehicle led to his discovery.

January 7, 2014, Needles District: A man suffered life-threatening injuries in a fall off a snow-covered cliff. His wife became stranded trying to contact her husband and almost fell down as well. A helicopter rescue was used.

March 20, 2019, Green River overlook: A missing thirty-three-year-old Iowa man was found dead at the base of a five-hundred-foot overlook. He had been reported missing on March 12.

July 29, 2021, Druid Arch: A sixty-six-year-old hiker became lost for four days on a ten-and-eight-tenths-mile trail to the arch. He was able to get water from other hikers but got lost again and had to drink water from puddles. A helicopter was dispatched, and he was rescued

May 12, 2022, Island in the Sky: Kevin Cox, sixty-three, of Spanish Fork, Utah, was found dead below the rim at Grand View Point. His death was likely caused by a fall, as his vehicle had been abandoned at Grand View Point.

July 19, 2022, Elephant Hill: A hiker was found deceased near the trailhead. He had been reported overdue. Extreme summer temperatures were the likely cause of his death.

49

DISASTERS IN CAPITOL REEF
NATIONAL PARK

March 21, 1993, Meek's Mesa: Three Colorado College students were reported stranded. They had shorts, little water and no overnight gear. They were able to start a fire and had to spend the night. The next day, they were rescued from a steep-walled mesa.

April 6, 1994, Burrow Wash: An overdue party of sixteen Boy Scouts was reported. Temperatures were expected to plunge at night. The boys were found the next day. They had started a fire to stay warm.

March 17, 1998, remote canyon: A woman slipped while traversing slickrock and fell into a water-filled pothole and broke her ankle. Her companion spent the night with her and then hiked out for help. When rescuers returned, she was in shock and hypothermic. It took two and a half hours to carry her out to a road and then a three-hour drive to a medical clinic.

May 22, 1998, Waterpocket Fold: Two men were traversing a steep, unnamed canyon when one of the men slipped and fell twenty feet, dislodging boulders on the way down. A three-hundred-pound boulder landed on the man's leg. His companion was able to free him, but both of his legs were injured. The companion had to hike out of the backcountry and drive thirty-five miles to summon help. A technical rescue involving a helicopter was needed. One of the man's feet was nearly severed, and he required multiple surgeries.

July 4, 1998, Fremont River: A twenty-year-old Bicknell, Utah man jumped off a waterfall and into the river, breaking a leg in two places. He

A tourist and a park ranger highlight an entrance sign in Capitol Reef, probably in the 1940s. *Courtesy of Utah State Historical Society.*

A group of young adults traverse a narrow gorge in Capitol Reef, probably in the 1940s. *Courtesy of Utah State Historical Society.*

A man is stranded in a boat during a flash flood in Capitol Reef National Park in 1943. *Courtesy of Utah State Historical Society.*

was unaware that the river was only three feet deep. Alcohol was also a factor in the accident.

June 27, 2002, Halls Creek: Six members of a church group were reported lost and dehydrated in the drainage of a remote backcountry route. Rescuers finally saw their light in the evening darkness. The group had failed to get a trip permit or obtain adequate information on their route, and they lit an illegal fire. But they were able to filter drinking water.

March 15, 2003, Spring Canyon: Four Boy Scouts and three adult leaders were backpacking a route that requires fording the Fremont River. But with record warmth, heavy snow was melting and raising the river significantly. Park rangers rushed to find the group, and they were advised not to cross. But they were too tired to return the way they had hiked in. One by one, with rescuers' help, they were able to use a safety line and, with helmets and lifejackets, successfully forded the river.

May 6, 2011, Chimney Rock: A fifty-seven-year-old man had fallen some twenty feet and suffered significant injuries. A satellite signal alerted park rangers, and help was dispatched. The man had a dislocated hip, three broken ribs and several skull fractures. Thirteen park staff were involved in the rescue.

May 25, 2019, Mulie Twist Trail: Three hikers had to be rescued after they became cold and fatigued during a rainstorm. Their hike had begun on May 22, and they were rescued a day after calling for help. It required an air search to find the hikers, and they were safely extracted.

50

TRAGEDIES IN ZION NATIONAL PARK

T here have been forty fatalities in falls and drownings in Zion National Park, including fourteen drownings, and eleven deaths in the Zion Narrows. There have been fourteen deaths in Angels Landing and three fatalities in the Emerald Pools area.

June 27, 1927, Cathedral Mountain: W.H.W. Evans of Pasadena, California, slid down a one-thousand-foot slope on the mountain and lay injured for some thirty-six hours before being found by park rangers. He was delirious but did survive with many cuts, bruises and a concussion.

April 11, 1930, Zion Valley: Albin Brooksby was killed in the park, on the valley floor, during a freak accident. An old metal rod on the cable apparatus that formerly lifted materials at Cable Mountain came loose, fell some three hundred feet down the mountain and struck Brooksby in the head.

Brooksby, the principal of Orderville Elementary School, was with a group of students and teachers at the time. In fact, he had warned some students to stop swinging on the metal cable hanging from the mountain moments before the accident. Their swinging likely loosened the metal bar high above them.

Two students, Devin Tait, eight, and Leon Stevens, ten, were also injured, along with several other students, but none seriously.

July 15, 1930, Mount Bryan: Eugene Cafferata, nineteen, of St. Louis, died from a fifty-five-foot fall in Zion National Park. It was believed that he fell over a cliff after trying to descend from Mount Bryan at nightfall. It is also likely that he was alive for many hours after the accident, as his

The remains of Cable Mountain, part of an early mining operation in Zion National Park. *Courtesy of Utah State Historical Society.*

body was not found for more than two days and exposure and shock likely caused his death.

July 25, 1931, Cathedral Mountain: Don Orcutt, twenty-four, of Los Angeles, fell some one thousand feet to his death in an accident in Zion National Park while climbing the mountain near West Rim Trail. His body was mangled almost beyond recognition.

Although Orcutt had been the first to climb the Great White Throne, a feat he accomplished a few weeks earlier, on June 30, his next Zion climb was fatal. He climbed with no ropes and with bare feet, as his Cathedral Mountain climb was just a warmup for an ascent up West Temple Mountain, considered far more dangerous. Orcutt had earlier reported that he fell some fifty feet during his climb up the Great White Throne but was able to stop himself from suffering a much longer fall.

Orcutt had also reported that he found a portion of a human skull during his climb up the Great White Throne. This is believed to be prehistoric evidence that at least one other person, possibly a Native American, had perished trying to scale the monolith.

September 4, 1951, Deer Trap Mountain: Lane Kelton Cottrell, seventeen, of Salt Lake City, died from a 50-foot-fall off the mountain in Zion National Park. He was hiking with two other friends but became separated from them. It is believed that he fell in the dark, after nightfall. His body was found the next day, about ten hours later, lodged 1,500 feet above the Zion Canyon floor.

September 17, 1961, Zion Narrows: Four Murray, Utah Boy Scouts and one adult leader were killed in a flash flood in the Narrows.

October 16, 1983, Emerald Pools: John Russell, nineteen, a Dixie College student from Ogden, died as a result of a fall from the Middle Emerald Pool in the park. He was scrambling off the established trail and lost his footing along an exposed edge.

April 1987, Angels Landing: A Denver, Colorado woman slipped and fell 250 feet to her death during the final climb up Angels Landing.

May 18, 1987, Scout Lookout, Angels Landing: A woman lost her footing (there is speculation that she tripped on the long dress she was wearing) as she was hiking with her husband and two others. She fell 250 vertical feet. Park personnel responded to the report. They performed CPR for one and a half hours. She was pronounced dead of massive internal injuries.

Two tourists on horseback greet two other horsemen in Zion National Park in the 1930s. *Courtesy of Utah State Historical Society.*

April 1989, Angels Landing: Jeff R. Dwyer, twenty-eight, of Sandpoint, Idaho, fell or jumped 150 feet on the Angels Landing trail and perished. It is unknown if it was an accident or a suicide.

June 20, 1990, Hidden Canyon: Seasonal park ranger John Ethridge, forty, was killed when he lost his footing on a trail in the canyon and fell off a cliff. Ethridge had finished leading a group on a nature hike at 10:30 a.m. When he turned to address the group, a rock slipped from under his feet, causing him to fall more than 150 feet to his death. Park personnel reached the body about an hour later, and Ethridge was pronounced dead at that time.

May 30, 1991, Virgin River: An eighteen-month-old child from Las Vegas drowned in the Virgin River, near the Watchman Campground. The body was found two hundred yards downstream from where the boy was last seen.

May 29, 1992, Zion Narrows: A large storm produced intense hail, wind and rain, causing the Virgin River to rise by more than seven feet. Twenty-five hikers were stranded in the Narrows. Park rangers rescued hikers, treated six for hypothermia and evacuated two campgrounds.

August 11, 1992, Hidden Canyon: A twenty-eight-year-old hiker from New Haven, Connecticut, fell approximately twenty-five vertical feet and suffered head, face and leg injuries while in the canyon. A twenty-person rescue team responded, and it took eight hours for the rescue due to the narrowness of the area and darkness. The person was treated and released from a local hospital.

October 10, 1992, Left Fork of North Creek: A thirty-two-year-old Salt Lake City man died after a 30-foot fall while rappelling. The rescue was in a 20-foot-wide narrow canyon with 150-foot vertical walls. A U.S. Air Force paramedic was lowered to the scene. The climber still had a pulse but later died at a St. George hospital.

May 14, 1993, South Fork, Taylor Canyon, Kolob area: A dead man was found by other hikers. He had apparently perished about thirty-six hours prior when he fell some one thousand feet.

July 15, 1993, Kolob Creek, adjacent to park boundaries: Two Salt Lake men drowned in separate incidents on private property. They were part of an Explorer Scout group on a four-day trek.

November 22, 1994, Court of the Patriarchs: A thirty-five-year-old man from Crested Butte, Colorado, fell about one hundred feet to his death while descending from a climb. Darkness is thought to have been a contributing factor.

May 16, 1995, Pine Creek Canyon: Three nineteen-year-old men rappelled into the canyon and became stranded after they were not prepared

A man uses his large camera to scan the mountainside in Zion National Park in the 1930s. *Courtesy of Utah State Historical Society.*

for rising waters in the narrow canyon. During their rescue, a thunderstorm struck as they were being lifted out of the canyon, filling it with water. They would have drowned if not rescued.

January 2, 1997, Angels Landing: A thirty-six-year-old Provo man fell eight hundred feet to his death while solo rock climbing the "Prodigal Sun" route. Recovery efforts were hampered by severe flooding, and removing the body required an innovative and complex procedure. During that recovery, park rangers had to rescue four different hikers on the East Rim Trail who were trapped by snow.

March 28, 1997, Emerald Pools: A twelve-year-old boy fell about one hundred feet to his death at the lower pool. The boy was wading in the pool and ventured too close to the cliff edge and slipped.

May 9, 1997, Observation Point Trail: A thirty-six-year-old woman from Medford, New Jersey, fell five hundred feet to her death. There were no witnesses.

May 26, 1997, Hidden Canyon: A twenty-four-year-old man fell fifty feet in the canyon and suffered serious injuries from multiple fractures. It took seven hours and thirteen rescuers to extract the man

September 14, 1997, Zion Narrows: A twenty-seven-year-old man from Flagstaff, Arizona, was hiking the Narrows alone when he noticed a rush of water. He turned around and sprinted one hundred yards to a small side drainage. There he found refuge from the rising waters but had to spend the night there. He was lightly dressed but managed to build a fire. The next morning, he was able to swim and hike out, with no injuries.

July 27, 1998, Zion Narrows: Two hikers drowned in the Virgin River while hiking the Narrows when a flash flood struck. The deceased were a twenty-seven-year-old Long Beach, California man and a thirty-one-year-old Paramont, California man. Seven other hikers were stranded in the Narrows overnight and alerted rangers to having seen a floating body.

August 1, 1998, Hidden Canyon: A twenty-seven-year-old man from Palisade, Colorado, fell thirty feet while scrambling in the canyon and was seriously injured. It took his hiking company ninety minutes to hike out and alert rangers. Since a carry out would have taken four hours, a helicopter was requested. But the man went into cardiac arrest five hours after the fall and died just before the copter arrived.

November 14, 1998, Cable Mountain: A forty-two-year-old Las Vegas woman became lost as she descended the mountain. She ended up in a slot canyon and had to swim through several pools of water. Her daughter was at a motel in Springdale and reported the mother missing. After a cold night on a rock ledge, the woman was found by rangers, who warmed her up and helped her hike out. Four technical lifts were required to get her back on the main trail.

December 27, 1998, Moonlight Buttress: Two men were doing a technical climb on this rock face when one of the men fell some thirty feet and sustained a major head injury. (He was not wearing a helmet.) The other man was able to make contact with another climbing group, and they got ranger help—a four-man team. The man was eventually flown to a Las Vegas hospital in critical condition.

January 21, 1999, Mountain of the Sun: A twenty-year-old Springdale woman was on a technical canyoneering route when she fell 150 feet off a rope to her death. Eventually, a five-hour recovery operation was able to retrieve the body.

October 2, 1999, Imlay Canyon: A twenty-seven-year-old woman scrambling in the West Rim area fell more than one hundred feet near Potato Hollow. She fractured both ankles. A rescue team arrived at dark and extracted the woman. She was eventually sent by helicopter to a Las Vegas hospital.

August 2, 2000, Angels Landing: A sixty-two-year-old German hiker died after he fell fifteen feet while going off-trail at Angels Landing. His body was removed by helicopter.

September 24, 2000, Eglestead Hollow: A forty-eight-year-old man became stranded two hundred feet below the rim of the hollow. He lacked the proper equipment, and his guidebook did not contain adequate

The main road in Zion National Park in the 1930s was a two-lane dirt highway. *Courtesy of Utah State Historical Society.*

information. The park's technical team was helicoptered in to rescue the uninjured man.

October 8, 2000, Grasshopper climbing area: A thirty-three-year-old man was rappelling and fell twenty feet and slid another thirty feet. He suffered a severe head injury and fractures. His companion flagged down a park shuttle and summoned help.

October 10, 2000, Pine Creek Canyon: Four men between the ages of thirty and fifty had to be rescued when thunderstorms produced a flash flood that trapped the men in a drainage area. Their cries for help were heard and reported to park dispatch. They were rescued via a tag line on the other side of the drainage area. As there had been a 60 percent chance of thunderstorms that day, the leader of the group was issued a citation for creating a hazardous condition.

July 14, 2001, Zion Subway: A rescue was conducted for a group of visitors stranded in the Subway. The group was unprepared for the technical and water issues on the adventure. The same day, a seventeen-year-old boy fell one hundred feet near the Emerald Pools. He had to be carried out to a waiting ambulance. As park personnel were involved in that rescue, they discovered that the victim's thirteen-year-old brother was stranded on a nearby cliff. He had to be rappelled down to safety.

April 22, 2001, Pine Creek: Three stranded climbers had to be rescued with a one-hundred-foot lift to the rim. They were cited for failing to obtain a canyoneering permit.

May 13, 2001, Canyon Overlook Trail: A ten-year-old Las Vegas boy fell some 150 feet to his death during a storm while hiking the trail with family and friends. Additional storms delayed recovering the body by several hours.

May 16, 2001, Left Fork of North Creek: A thirty-seven-year-old woman from Beaumont, Texas, perished in a fifty-foot fall when she went off-trail. Her two fellow hikers eventually found her lying unresponsive, but no one had witnessed her fall.

July 4, 2001, Angels Landing Trail: An eighteen-year-old man fell twenty feet on the trail and was found unconscious by other hikers. It required a twenty-five-person team and a helicopter to extract him.

January 3, 2002, Refrigerator Canyon: A thirty-six-year-old man had to be rescued coming down from Angels Landing. He and a group of friends were tossing a Frisbee around when it landed off-trail. The man tried to retrieve it and fell thirty feet. A seven-person team evacuated the man, who had a fracture of his vertebra.

Visitors on horseback are shown on the very cliffy West Rim Trail of Zion National Park in the 1930s. *Courtesy of Utah State Historical Society.*

May 21, 2002, Zion Canyon: A thirty-five-year-old man from Bournemouth, England, fell 180 feet to his death while attempting the "Spaceshot" technical climb on the east end of the canyon, between Big Bend and Temple of Sinawaya.

June 1, 2002, Pine Creek: A fifty-one-year-old man fell the final twenty feet of a one-hundred-foot rappel in Pine Canyon after he lost control. He had to be raised six hundred feet to the canyon rim and then carried a mile to the Zion Highway. The man had a fractured leg, rope burns and other injuries.

July 23, 2002, Subway: A nineteen-year-old man had to be rescued after he fell thirty feet and fractured his right leg. Because of darkness, rescuers had to stay with the injured man overnight. The next day, a four-hundred-foot guiding line was used to raise him above the rim to a waiting helicopter.

January 21, 2003, Scout Lookout: The body of a sixty-six-year-old woman from Joshua Tree, California, was found after a fatal fall in the area.

March 25, 2003, Angels Landing: A fifty-nine-year-old woman had to be rescued after a fall on the Angels Landing trail fractured her hip. Seventeen persons were involved in the rescue, and a helicopter had to be summoned from the Grand Canyon to lift her to an ambulance.

August 17, 2003, Angels Landing: A hiker who suffered head and arm injuries after a ten-foot fall on the trail had to be rescued with a helicopter from the Grand Canyon.

September 5, 2003, Behunin Canyon: A thirty-seven-year-old Springdale, Utah man who had been reported as missing was found dead after a sixty-to-ninety-foot fall while rappelling. On the same day, a raft was used to evacuate an eleven-year-old boy out of the Zion Narrows. He had significant leg injuries from a fall there.

June 25, 2004, Angels Landing: A fourteen-year-old Boy Scout from Long Beach, California, fell some one thousand feet to his death. The boy had gone off-trail and was attempting to scratch his name in a cliff as part of a five-dollar bet when he lost his footing.

August 20, 2005, Englestead Canyon: A thirty-two-year-old man had to be rescued when a one-hundred-pound rock fell off the canyon wall and partially amputated his big toe. A six-hundred-foot lift into and out of the canyon was required.

January 1, 2006, Park's east side: A thirty-six-year-old man suffered a forty-foot-fall into a drainage next to a road. He was unable to move and suffered back injuries.

May 31, 2006, Heaps Canyon: A man suffering from hypothermia had to be rescued. His group of three did not use maps or wet suits during their rappelling, and they made wrong turns and became trapped. The other men were able to escape on their own after new equipment was dropped to them.

June 20, 2006, four rescues: (1) A woman who broke her ankle had to be rescued off Angels Landing. (2) A hiker with chest pains had to be taken out of the Zion Narrows. (3) A trio of men rappelling in Echo Canyon, above Weeping Rock, had to be rescued after becoming stranded because of insufficient rope. (4) A man with an injured knee had to be rescued from the Zion Narrows.

August 22, 2006, Angels Landing: A twenty-nine-year-old Las Vegas woman fell to her death some 1,200 feet off Angels Landing.

October 25, 2006, Wildcat Canyon: A fifty-five-year-old hiker from Virginia was rescued in the Kolob Terrace area after he fell about one hundred feet down a slope and dislocated his shoulder.

June 4, 2007, Upper Emerald Pools area: A forty-eight-year-old Garden Grove, California man fell to his death during a 285-foot rappel in the Heaps Canyon area. His two companions reported him missing, and rangers later found his body.

June 8, 2007, Angels Landing: A fifty-three-year-old St. Louis man died from a one-thousand-foot fall while hiking the area about halfway between Scout Lookout and the summit.

June 20, 2008, Shelf Canyon: An eighteen-year-old man became stuck while climbing one hundred vertical feet without ropes or equipment. The next day, park rangers had to rescue a canyoneering party of four who had become stranded.

June 25, 2008, Subway: A thirty-nine-year-old man injured a leg during an uneven jump. He was later rescued by helicopter.

July 30, 2008, Pine Creek: A backcountry volunteer fell one hundred feet while rappelling. A helicopter rescued the woman, who was in serious condition.

October 17, 2008, Touchstone canyoneering route: A thirty-four-year-old Durango, Colorado man fell three hundred feet to his death on a popular climbing route across from Angels Landing.

November 29, 2008, Park's east entrance: A fifty-five-year-old Salt Lake City man died when he fell about twenty feet while hiking a side canyon near the Highway 9 entrance. Rangers arrived on the scene just twelve minutes after the accident.

April 24, 2009, Zion Narrows: Two kayakers required assistance after they lost their boats in the Narrows during the short time that kayaks can legally be used there. They had to spend an unplanned night there and then tried to climb their way out, then became stranded on a ledge eight hundred feet above the river. A helicopter eventually rescued them.

May 9, 2009, Pine Creek Canyon: A twenty-seven-year-old man had to be rescued on the "Feast of Snakes" climbing route after he fell twenty feet on a

A man stands atop his horse while traversing a narrow section of the East Rim Trail in the 1920s. *Courtesy of Utah State Historical Society.*

rappel and suffered fractures. A Blackhawk helicopter from Nellis Air Force Base was used to rescue him.

August 9, 2009, Angels Landing: A fifty-five-year-old woman from Glendora, California, died from a one-thousand-foot fall. Rescuers rappelled to recover the body.

November 27, 2009, Angels Landing: A fifty-year-old Pocatello, Idaho woman fell to her death off Angels Landing.

April 25, 2010, Zion Narrows: Two rafters drowned in the Virgin River. The pair lacked wet suits or experience in whitewater rafting. The men were trying to float some fifty miles from the Narrows to Hurricane, Utah, and videotape the experience as an entry in a TV competition.

April 27, 2010, Angels Landing: Regine Milobedzki, sixty-three, of Upland, California, fell one thousand feet to his death near Scout Lookout.

April 30, 2010, Pine Creek Canyon: A climber who was hanging upside-down had to be rescued during a one-hundred-foot rappel that went wrong.

May 16, 2010, Hidden Canyon: A fifty-year-old woman injured both arms during a twenty-foot fall. A four-hundred-foot-long highline was required to rescue her the next morning.

July 28–29, 2010, Subway and Spry Canyon: Two rescues were required in two days. A sixty-one-year-old Salt Lake man was rescued from the Subway with a fractured ankle. The next day, after a severe thunderstorm, three hikers were injured as they were flushed out of Spry Canyon and suffered life-threatening injuries. Three helicopters were required for the rescue.

September 19, 2010, Subway: A twenty-year-old hiker from Boise, Idaho, had to be rescued after a ten-foot jump injured her ankle. Rangers discourage such jumping in the Subway around obstacles, but it continues to happen.

April 17, 2011, Subway: Nine hikers had to be rescued after they had trouble getting through some of the technical areas of the Subway. None were injured, but locating them was a lengthy process.

May 21, 2011, Angels Landing: Two different hikers required rescue on the trail. One, a twenty-four-year-old man from Norway, had a leg fracture after he jumped five feet off a pinnacle on the route. Another man, a sixty-two-year-old from St. George, Utah, had collapsed halfway up due to chest pains.

June 8, 2011, Hidden Canyon: A thirty-year-old man from the Netherlands fell ten feet onto his head while down-climbing a slickrock in the canyon. A technical rescue involving twenty-seven park staff was required because of the difficult terrain.

July 16, 2011, two separate rescues, one in Mystery Canyon and another in the Narrows: A twenty-year-old man suffered a leg fracture while descending into Mystery Canyon. His rescue out of the deep gully required six hours of help from park rangers. A thirty-seven-year-old man sustained knee and leg injuries in the Narrows and had to spend the night there. The next day, park staff spent six hours carrying him out.

July 17, 2011, Imlay Canyon: Two canyoneers in a group of seven required park ranger assistance after they became injured when their anchors failed. A twenty-year-old man fell 10 feet and suffered leg injuries. Soon after, a woman in the group fell 140 feet, but the friction of the ropes likely saved her life. She suffered a shattered ankle. A helicopter from Grand Canyon was used to rescue her. The injured man was hoisted to safety and then carried out. The group faced wilderness permit violations.

July 19, 2011, Angels Landing: One hour after dark, flashing lights and shouts for help came from a cliff just below Angels Landing. One man had suffered a head injury in a fall, and the group's ropes were damaged. Another climber had fallen and suffered hand injuries. Both had to be rescued with the assist of a helicopter and had to be lowered six hundred feet to the canyon floor.

November 15, 2011, Jolly Gulch: A woman fell sixty feet while free-climbing and suffered multiple fractures and lacerations. She was rescued with ropes and a helicopter. The uninjured man in the two-person climbing party was issued a citation for failing to obtain a canyoneering wilderness permit.

July 1, 2012, Moonlight Buttress/Minotaur Tower: A man fell forty feet and had to survive the night with multiple injuries before the sun came up and rangers were able to retrieve him.

June 29, 2013, Birch Hollow: A twenty-one-year-old woman fell as much as sixty feet and suffered a hip fracture and some internal injuries in a climb just outside the park boundaries. An emergency team spent the night with the woman, and a haul and helicopter lift extracted her the next day. Later that day, a twenty-one-year-old woman suffered spinal and leg injuries in a twenty-foot fall on the same route as the prior day's accident. She also required helicopter extraction.

July 8, 2013, Heaps Canyon: Three canyoneers had to be rescued after they became stranded, facing an unexpected thirty-foot-high obstacle.

July 25, 2013, Zion Lodge area: A park concessions employee died after a fifty-foot fall on "Employee Falls." The twenty-two-year-old man from Florida was walking near the edge when he lost his footing and slipped.

September 2, 2013, Behuin Canyon: A thirty-three-year-old Arizona man rappelling fell about fifty feet and suffered head, arm, leg and back injuries. A rescue squad from Nellis Air Force Base was called and extracted the man by helicopter. A doctor at a Las Vegas hospital, where the man was taken, reported that, due to the extent of his injuries, survival overnight in Zion would have been impossible.

September 6, 2013, Angels Landing: A twenty-three-year-old man was hiking off-route when he slid some thirty feet and suffered a head laceration and other injuries. Park personnel stayed with the man overnight, and he was hauled out the next day.

March 11, 2014, Jolly Gulch: A canyoneer fell thirty feet and was severely injured along the park's eastern boundary. Despite erratic winds, the man was rescued by helicopter. He had not been wearing a helmet.

October 27, 2014, Zion Narrows: A man drowned after being stranded overnight by rain and high water flow in the Virgin River. His companion had swum out safely earlier. The man's body was found about a mile downstream from where he had been last seen.

Visitors rest beneath the Three Patriarchs formation in Zion National Park in the 1930s. *Courtesy of Utah State Historical Society.*

October 10, 2014, Pine Creek and Hidden Canyon: Rangers had to conduct two simultaneous rescues. A thirty-five-year-old canyoneer jumped into a pool of water and expected the water to cushion his fall, but he broke his leg. Separately, a fifty-one-year-old woman broke her leg in Hidden Canyon. A total of twenty-five personnel were involved in the two rescues.

Park rangers say that jumping, as opposed to rope- or down-climbing, is the leading cause of preventable injuries in the park.

October 19, 2014, Iron Messiah Climb, near the Zion Lodge: A forty-seven-year-old California climber died after an eight-foot fall. His was the eighth climbing fatality in the park since 1983.

April 20, 2015, Pine Creek: An injured man had to be rescued from this technical slot canyon, where wet suits and multiple rappels are required. He suffered a broken ankle. Five hours were required for the rescue.

March 4, 2017, Angels Landing: Tate Ryan Volino, forty-five, of Osprey, Florida, died in a fall off the south side of Angels Landing.

May 18, 2017, Weeping Rock: A man in his twenties had to be rescued from a cliff several hundred feet above the Weeping Rock Trail after he became stranded.

June 6, 2017, Lady Mountain: A hiker slid one hundred feet into a narrow rock ravine. His rescue required two hours.

June 20–21, 2017, Wildcat Canyon, West Rim and Emerald Pools: Three separate rescues were required for injured hikers. A man on the Wildcat Trail fell out of a tree and injured his ankle. A man on the West Rim Trail had chest pains and required medical attention. Later, a man had similar issues in the Emerald Pools area.

February 5, 2018, Refrigerator Canyon: A woman's body was found along the West Rim Trail. Her injuries were consistent with a fall from Angels Landing.

March 17, 2018, Pine Creek: Eight people were rescued from this slot canyon by a team of sixteen. They were tired and cold and some likely would not have survived the snow and cold overnight. The group lacked adequate footwear, gloves and wet suits.

June 3, 2018, Riverside Walk Trail: A rare rockfall injured two hikers along the paved trail. They were treated at the scene and taken to a medical facility.

July 30, 2018, Subway: Hikers in two separate groups needed rescuing. One man was unable to move after injuring a knee, and the second group became lost. The first group ignored park ranger advice to take ropes along while securing their trip permits. A log that was in place a year prior was gone, and a man in the group jumped down and injured his leg. The second group had inadequate footwear for the Subway.

August 28, 2018, Hidden Canyon: Six hikers became trapped when a rockfall struck in the canyon. No one was injured, but they were rescued by a helicopter that arrived from the Grand Canyon. The canyon was closed for a week.

A wagon hauls visitors around Zion National Park, probably in the 1950s. *Courtesy of Utah State Historical Society.*

February 16, 2019, Left Fork of North Creek: In a rare situation, a thirty-four-year-old Arizona man was trapped when his leg became stuck in quicksand in a creek pool. A woman with him was able to hike three hours to get cellphone reception and notify park rangers. It required two hours to free the man's leg. When darkness fell, rescuers and the man had to spend the night in the area, with four inches of new snow falling. A helicopter extracted the man the next day.

April 18, 2019, Angels Landing: A thirty-five-year-old woman fell to her death on the Angels Landing trail. After she was reported missing, her body was found days later. It was determined that she died from a high-elevation fall.

June 14, 2019, Virgin River: Three people had to be rescued from the swift-flowing river. A twelve-year-old boy who was wading was swept away, and a mother and a second woman went after him. The mother was able to put the boy on a large boulder. All were eventually rescued without injury.

July 22, 2019, Subway: A forty-eight-year-old man suffering from overexertion had to be rescued from the Subway. He had to stay there overnight until rangers could reach him.

August 24, 2019, Weeping Rock: A substantial piece of rock broke off Cable Mountain and showered down some three thousand feet below to Weeping Rock, injuring three people.

November 21, 2019, Angels Landing: A park concession employee was found dead at the bottom of Angels Landing. Nineteen-year-old Savannah McTague from Maine had fatal injuries consistent with a high-elevation fall.

March 4, 2021, Angels Landing: Jason Hartwell, forty-three, of Draper, Utah, died in a fall from the summit.

September 15, 2021, Zion Narrows: A rockfall just beyond the end of the Riverside Walk injured a woman walking in the Virgin River. She was treated at a St. George hospital.

November 27, 2021, Heaps Canyon: A man rappelling overshot his mark by twenty feet and was suspended. His two companions eventually got help the next morning, but by then their teammate had perished.

January 10, 2022, Hop Valley: A backpacker became stuck in three feet of snow but was able to use a satellite device to call for help. Her legs became numb, but she was rescued and treated for hypothermia.

May 1, 2022, Kolob Canyon Road: A thirty-five-year-old solo hiker had scrambled up a cliff face above the main park road. He fell thirty feet during his descent but caught himself on a small ledge with a bush. He spent twelve hours there with ankle injuries before being rescued.

August 19, 2022, Zion Narrows: A twenty-nine-year-old man drowned after flash flooding in the Narrows. He did not know how to swim and was reported missing by family members. His body was found three days later about six miles south of the Narrows.

BIBLIOGRAPHY

Chapter 1

Information gathered during a May 18, 2021 Kanarraville Falls hike.
Kanarra Falls. https://www.kanarrafalls.com.

Chapter 2

Ephraim (UT) Enterprise. October 2, 1936.
Information gathered during a May 16, 2021 hike in Box Canyon.

Chapter 3

Deseret News (Salt Lake City, UT). March 30, 1963.
Zimmerman, Dean R. "The Salt Lake Temple." *New Era* (June 1978).

Chapter 4

Roberts, B.H. *A Comprehensive History of the Church of Jesus Christ of the Latter-day Saints*.
    Salt Lake City, UT: Church of Jesus Christ of the Latter-day Saints, 1930.
Smith, George A. Address given in the "new" tabernacle on June 20, 1869.
Smith, Joseph S. Address given in the Provo Tabernacle on December 3, 1882.
Wright, Dennis A., and Rebekah E. Westrup. "Ensign Peak." Brigham Young
    University, Religious Studies Center. https://rsc.byu.edu.

Chapter 5

Provo (UT) Daily Herald. "At Four Corners. Needed: Visitor Center, Park." July 6, 1972.
    ———. "Four Corners 'Incredible Disgrace'—Lawmakers." May 19, 1982.
Salt Lake Tribune (Salt Lake City, UT). "Obscure, Perilous Dirt Route Trap for
    Intrepid Tourists." December 22, 1957.

Bibliography

Chapter 6

Ogden (UT) Standard-Examiner. "500 Trek to Willard Peak." July 18, 1939.
———. February 2, 1941.
———. July 22, 1948.
———. September 27, 1970.

Chapter 7

Russell, Osborne. Diary, 1834–43. Library of Western Fur Trade Historical Source
    Documents. http://user.xmission.com/~drudy/mtman/html/ruslintr.html.

Chapter 8

Salt Lake Telegram (Salt Lake City, UT). July 24, 1921.

Chapter 9

Davis County Clipper (Woods Cross, UT). November 13–14, 1901.
Deseret News. September 21, 1859.
———. October 21, 1868.
Salt Lake Republican (Salt Lake City, UT). December 6, 1871.

Chapter 10

Davis County Clipper, May 23, 1914
Salt Lake Republican, August 22, 1873.
Utah's Dixie. www.utahsdixie.info.
Van Cott, John W. *Utah Place Names.* Salt Lake City: University of Utah Press, 1990.

Chapter 11

Union Pacific (Spring 1924).
Washington County (UT) News. December 25, 1924.

Chapter 12

Iron County (UT) Record. August 21, 1929.
———. September 25, 1941.
Iron County Register. August 29, 1913.
Salt Lake Telegram. "Upper Zion Has Greatest Thrill, Declares Party." August 24, 1925.
Zion National Park. www.zionnationalpark.net.

Chapter 13

Deseret News. "The Twin Peaks. Three Gentlemen Make the Ascent to the Summits."
    August 22, 1883.

———. November 5, 1897.

Salt Lake Herald. "Local Girls Climb Dizzy Twin Peaks." August 8, 1919.

———. November 3, 1897.

Salt Lake Telegram. July 30, 1912.

Chapter 14

Salt Lake Herald. July 26, 1871.

———. May 24, 1885.

———. November 4, 1913.

Salt Lake Telegram. "Keen Interest in Long Distance Runs." November 22, 1913.

———. April 5, 1902.

Salt Lake Tribune. "University Basket-Ball. Girls Defeat the Boys in the First Open Game." May 16, 1897.

———. "Williams Wins Marathon; Race Is Great Success." December 8, 1913.

———. December 18, 1871.

———. May 21, 1880

———. April 22, 1900.

———. October 9, 1916.

Chapter 15

Ogden Standard-Examiner. "One of Racing Airplanes Passes over Ogden, Causing a Craning of Many Necks." October 13, 1919.

Salt Lake Herald. "First Horseless Carriage Seen on Salt Lake Streets." April 13, 1899.

Chapter 16

Kaysville-Layton Historical Society. *Layton, Utah.* Layton, UT: Kaysville-Layton Historical Society, 1985.

McCormick, Nancy D., and John S. McCormick. *Saltair.* Sprinville, UT: Bonneville Books, 1985.

Utah History Encyclopedia. www.uen.org.

Chapter 17

Lutz, Susan Juch. "Cleaned Up and Cleaned Out: Ruined Hot Spring Resorts of Utah." *GHC Bulletin* (December 2004).

Pearce, Louise B. "Salt Lake City's Vanishing Hot Springs." Unpublished manuscript, Utah Historical Society, 1953.

Utah History Encyclopedia. www.uen.org.

Chapter 18

Information gathered during visits to Provo Canyon in May 1978 and June 1990.

Provo Canyon Parks. "Bridal Veil Falls Park." www.provo-canyon-parks.weebly.com.

Provo Daily Herald. "Bridal Veil Tram Line Cut Down." August 13, 2008.
Wein, Marc Jonathan. "The Legend and History of Bridal Veil Falls." Intermountain Histories. https://www.intermountainhistories.org.

Chapter 19

Carter, Edward L."Timp Path Began Hike to Popularity 85 Years Ago." *Deseret News,* July 13, 1997.
———. "Timp Roberts." *Y Magazine* (Fall 1998).
Wein, Marc Jonathan. "Eugene 'Timp' Roberts' Annual Timpanogos Hike." Intermountain Histories. https://www.intermountainhistories.org.

Chapter 20

Manti Messenger. July 31, 1925.
Salt Lake Herald. "Aloft on Mount Nebo; Utah Peak Has Beauty of Alps; Grandeur in View." March 1, 1920.

Chapter 21

Mormon Encyclopedia. https://eom.byu.edu.
Salt Lake Telegram. September 17, 1910.
Salt Lake Tribune. March 9, 1911.

Chapter 22

Deseret Evening News (Salt Lake City, UT). May 16, 1908.
Salt Lake Telegram. October 15, 1930.

Chapter 23

Brigham City (UT) Bugler. August 1, 1890.
Davis County Clipper. August 26, 1910.
Salt Lake Herald. July 21, 1887.
———. August 25, 1889.
Salt Lake Times. August 31, 1892.

Chapter 24

Ashton, Marvin O. "The Last Leaf on the Tree." *Deseret News,* August 21, 1943.
Visit to Hooper, Utah cemetery, May 2021.

Chapter 25

Anderson, Justin. Interview with author, December 12, 2013. Anderson is an Ogden City engineer.

Ogden Standard-Examiner. March 25, 1888.
————. July 16, 1924.

Chapter 26

Hunter, Milton R. *Beneath Ben Lomond's Peak*. Salt Lake City, UT: Daughters of Utah
    Pioneers, Quality Press, 1995.
Ogden Standard-Examiner. "As Usual Zion Claims It All." April 5, 1911.
————. "Ogden Tabernacle Choir to Sing in Salt Lake Tabernacle Tomorrow."
    April 7, 1917.
————. "Presidency of Church Favors Ogden Choir." April 4, 1911.
————. "A Tabernacle Choir. It Was Thoroughly Organized Sunday Afternoon."
    March 10, 1891.

Chapter 27

Davis County Clipper. June 14, 1894; June 21, 1894.
————. September 12, 1952.
Salt Lake Herald. August 7, 1894.
Salt Lake Tribune. June 12, 1894.
————. June 24, 1894.

Chapter 28

Strack, Don. Utah Rails. www.utahrails.net.
Utah History Encyclopedia. www.uen.org.

Chapter 29

McCormick and McCormick, *Saltair*.
Utah History Encyclopedia. www.uen.org.
In-person interviews with Roger Pusey, March 1998.

Chapter 30

The Church of Jesus Christ of Latter-day Saints. Church History Library. 15 East
    North Temple Street, Salt Lake City, Utah. Accessed October 2009. https://
    history.churchofjesuschrist.org.
Mormon Encyclopedia. https://eom.byu.edu.

Chapter 31

Baker, Fred. Interview with author. Baker is a retired chairman of the LDS Church
    Building Department. Interview conducted at Baker's home, 3135 Tyler Avenue,
    Ogden, Utah, September 8, 2014.
Deseret News. May 16, 1921.

Ogden Standard-Examiner. "Ogden to Get Temple, Mormons Are Told." December 13, 1920.
———. May 7, 1924.

Chapter 32

American Fork (UT) Citizen. September 8, 1923.
Ogden Standard-Examiner. "Will Dynamite Crash Hilltop(?)" August 19, 1937.
Salt Lake Telegram. "Hikers Climb Peak to Set New Record." October 3, 1938.
———. "Wasatch Mountain Club Hikers Ascend Lone Peak." August 4, 1925.

Chapter 33

Ogden Standard-Examiner. "Reservoir Site Abandoned." November 22, 1912.
———. March 23, 1911.
———. May 18, 1923.

Chapter 34

Davis County Clipper. "Davis Urges Wider Road, Inter-Regional Highway." December 3, 1948.
Deseret News. July 17, 1996.

Chapter 35

Beaver County (UT) News. July 15, 1927.

Chapter 36

Ogden Standard-Examiner. "State Prison May Be Moved." September 28, 1922.

Chapter 37

Gunnison Valley News. February 8, 1934.
National Park Service. "Zion National Park." https://www.nps.gov.

Chapter 38

Deseret News. "Terrible Disaster. Terrific Explosion of Forty Tons of Giant, Hercules, Blasting and Other Powder. Four Persons Killed Instantly and Others Injured. Great Damage to Property." April 6, 1876.
Utah History Encyclopedia. www.uen.org.

Chapter 39

Deseret News. "Avalanche at Alta." March 12, 1884.
————. February 15, 1885.

Chapter 40

Deseret News. "Destroyed!; (Park) City Practically Wiped Out; A Raging Conflagration; Scene of Ruin and Despair." June 20, 1898.
Salt Lake Herald. "Park City Laid in Ashes Yesterday." June 20, 1898.
Van Leer, Twila. "1898 Conflagration Turned Park City into 'Fiery Furnace.'" *Deseret News,* January 7, 1996.

Chapter 41

Times News of Nephi (UT). "A Wall of Water. The City of Manti Swept by a Cloudburst. Streets Turned into a Raging River. Thousands of Dollars of Damage Done—No Lives Are Lost." July 14, 1899.

Chapter 42

Ogden Standard-Examiner. "Cloudburst Death Toll Mounts, Mangled Bodies Found in Debris; Scouts Victims." August 14, 1923.

Chapter 43

Pope, Dan, and Clayton Brough, eds. *Utah's Weather and Climate.* Salt Lake City, UT: Publisher's Press, 1996.
Various persons. Interviews with authors. Interviews with persons who lived during the winter of 1948–49. October 2013.

Chapter 44

Ogden Standard-Examiner. "Pacific Limited Crash Claims 48 Lives." January 1, 1945.
Strack, Don. Utah Rails. www.utahrails.net.

Chapter 45

Ogden Standard-Examiner. "Holdups Make No Effort to Resist Officers," January 14, 1911.
————. "Suspects Are to Leave the Jail." January 23, 1911.
————. "Train Held Up, One Man Killed and Passengers Robbed Just West of Ogden." January 3, 1911.

Chapter 46

Times Independent (Moab, UT). "Arkansas Man Died in Arches." May 25, 1978.

————. "Boy Injured in Canyonlands." August 11, 1972.
————. "California Visitor Dies on Canyonlands Tour." November 13, 1969.
————. "Four Accidents Reported in Arches during Week." April 6, 1972.
————. "Injured Hiker Rescued Sunday in Devils Garden in Country." August 11, 1997.
————. "Injured in Canyonlands." February 24, 1977.
————. "Man Hurt in Fall in Canyonlands." March 23, 1978.
————. "Pair Injured in Canyonlands Accident Saturday." June 29, 1978.
————. "Tourist Falls 400 Feet to His Death in Arches Monument." June 1, 1950.
————. "Woman Injured in Accident." September 18, 1969.

Chapter 47

Garfield County (UT) News. "Girl Dies in Fall at Bryce." June 14, 1979.
————. "Swiss Tot Dies in Bryce Canyon Fall." June 14, 1979.
————. "13-Year-Old Killed in Fall at Bryce Canyon." February 21, 1991.
————. "Tourist Dies in Fall at Bryce." April 22, 1954.
National Park Service. Bryce Canyon National Park. Incident report. http://npshistory.com/morningreport/incidents/brca.htm.
Salt Lake Telegram. "Bryce Tragedy Probe Opens at Panguitch." November 5, 1947.

Chapter 48

National Park Service. Canyonlands National Park. Incident report. http://npshistory.com/morningreport/incidents.
Times Independent. "Hiker Hurt in Fall in Canyonlands." March 23, 1978.

Chapter 49

National Park Service. Capitol Reef National Park. Incident report. http://npshistory.com/morningreport/incidents/care.htm.

Chapter 50

Garfield County News. July 18, 1930.
Iron County Record. July 29, 1931; August 19, 1931.
Kane County (UT) Standard. April 18, 1930
National Park Service. Zion National Park. Incident report. http://npshistory.com/morningreport/incidents/zion.htm.
Salt Lake Telegram. September 5, 1951.

ABOUT THE AUTHOR

L ynn Arave graduated from Weber State University with degrees in communications-journalism and human performance. He worked for the *Deseret News* for thirty-two years, first as a sportswriter, then as a feature writer and finally as a city desk reporter and editor. He is the author of the books *Walking Salt Lake City*, *Layton Utah* (Images of America), *Detour Utah: Mysteries, Legends and Peculiar Places* and the *Mystery of Utah History* blog. Lynn lives in Layton with his wife, LeAnn Flygare Arave.

Visit us at
www.historypress.com